UNLOCKING MODEL-DRIVEN ENGINEERING:
CONCEPTS, FOUNDATIONS, AND APPLICATIONS

Abdelkrim Mebarki

To my parents,
To my brothers and sisters,
To my teachers and my students,
To the person who has always supported me and without whom this work would never have been completed… To my wife and eternal soulmate.

Preface

This work is the result of several years of teaching in the Master's program in Information Systems and Data (ISD) at the Department of Computer Science of the University of Science and Technology of Oran (Mohamed Boudiaf) in Algeria. I have illustrated and expanded my lecture notes in order to broaden the range of readers beyond the students of this Master's program. I have enriched them with more examples, additional details, and other topics not covered in the course.

I hope that this modest work will be beneficial and of great interest to students and young researchers, as well as to the general public wishing to explore this field from its foundations, beyond the illustrations and the final use of commercially available products.

Contents

List of Figures and Tables

Chapter 1. Introduction to MDE

Natural evolution imposes a permanent change in concepts, ideas, tools and working methods. In search of greater efficiency and profitability, Informatics is constantly seeking to develop its working tools and its reflection mode. This is why, after the invention of the calculating machine, a whole discipline was created to deal only with thinking about how to create an application: Software engineering.

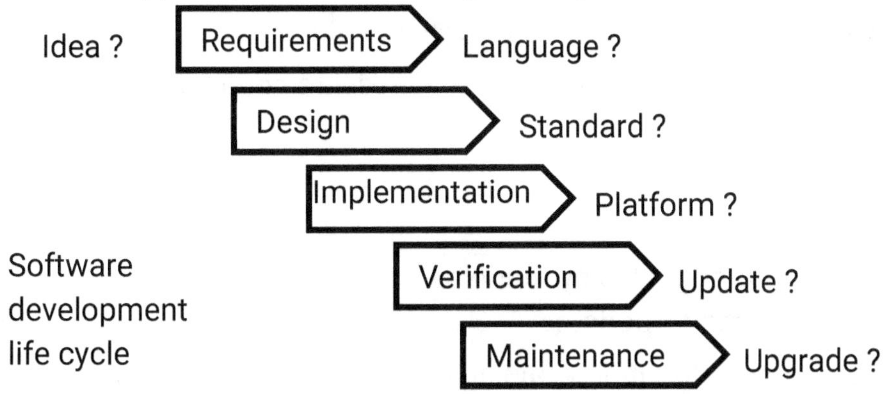

Figure 1 Classic software development life cycle

1.1 Understanding the MDE Concept: "Model" and "Engineering"

Model-Driven Engineering (MDE) is a software development paradigm that emphasizes the systematic use of models as primary artifacts throughout the engineering process. The MDE concept is deeply tied to its two constituent terms: Model and Engineering.

1.1.1 Engineering: The Process of Structured Problem Solving

In MDE, **Engineering** implies a disciplined, structured approach to solving complex problems. It involves several fundamental steps:

1.1.1.1 a. How to Reason?

Engineering requires analytical thinking and formal reasoning. This includes:

- Identifying constraints, goals, and variables.
- Using logical inference, deduction, and abstraction to analyze problems.

In MDE, models help structure and formalize this reasoning process.

1.1.1.2 b. How to Understand the Problem?

Understanding the problem entails:

- Building an abstract representation of the domain (a **domain model**).
- Gathering and interpreting requirements.
- Communicating with stakeholders through shared models.

MDE promotes early modeling to improve understanding and stakeholder communication.

1.1.1.3 c. How to Formulate the Solution?

Formulating a solution involves:

- Designing architecture, behaviors, and system components as models.
- Specifying how parts interact.

Model transformations and domain-specific modeling languages (DSMLs) enable solution formulation at a high abstraction level.

1.1.1.4 d. How to Implement?

Implementation in MDE is model-centric:

- Code is often **generated from models** via automatic transformations.
- Focus is placed on *what* the system should do, not *how*.

Executable models (e.g., in SysML or fUML) can be transformed into source code.

1.1.1.5 e. How to Apply?

Applying the engineered solution includes:

- Testing models and code.
- Deploying systems generated or guided by models.
- Evolving the system through model updates.

MDE ensures traceability from models to runtime, aiding maintenance and evolution.

1.1.2 Model: A Central Concept in Computer Science

In the **context** of MDE, a **model** is a simplified, abstract representation of a system or concept, created to better understand, design, and implement it.

1.1.2.1 a. What is the model in Computer Science ?

A model can represent:

- A **machine** (e.g., finite-state machine modeling software behavior).
- An **algorithm** (e.g., a data flow diagram showing computational steps).
- A **program** (e.g., a UML model representing object interactions).

In MDE, models are more abstract than source code but precise enough to support automation.

1.1.2.2 b. What is the Backbone of Computer Reasoning?

The backbone is:

- **Formal semantics**: rules that define how model elements behave.
- **Transformation rules**: mappings from model to model (e.g., platform-independent to platform-specific).
- **Meta-models**: models that define the structure and rules for other models.

Meta-modeling enables reasoning about models and guarantees model consistency and validity.

1.1.2.3 c. Formulate All of the Items in Terms of the Model Concept

All aspects of software engineering can be framed using models:

- **Requirements** → captured as requirement models.

- **Design** → expressed through structural (e.g., class diagrams) and behavioral (e.g., statecharts) models.
- **Code** → generated from models or described in model-like structures.
- **Testing** → modeled as test cases, test data, and test coverage models.
- **Deployment and configuration** → captured in deployment models.

MDE advocates a unified modeling approach across the software lifecycle.
In summary, Model-Driven Engineering rethinks software development around models. By treating models as **first-class citizens**, MDE improves:

- Productivity
- Maintainability
- Reusability
- Consistency

It also promotes **automation** and **formal reasoning**, aligning software development with principles of modern systems engineering.

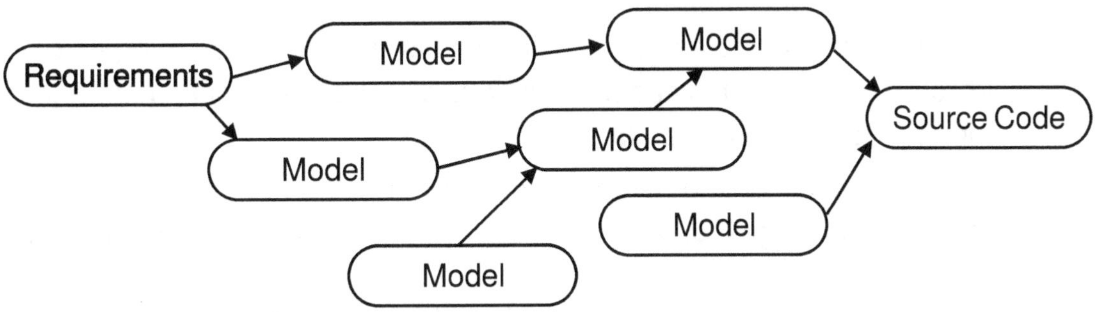

Figure 2 Model-based Software Development Process

1.1.3 MDE, the solution for project failure ?

According to statistics, up to 80% of IT projects fail at various stages (ranging from requirement definition to verification). This failure is due to several factors :

1. Poor Planning and Requirements Gathering. In this area, we can list many key elements:
    a. Lack of clear objectives – Unclear or undefined goals lead to misaligned efforts, wasted resources, and failure to deliver expected business value.
    b. Insufficient user involvement – Without early and continuous user feedback, the final product often fails to meet real needs, resulting in low adoption.
    c. Changing requirements throughout the project – Uncontrolled scope creep causes delays, budget overruns, and frustration as teams struggle to keep up with shifting demands.
    d. Inadequate communication – Poor information sharing creates misunderstandings, duplicated work, and overlooked dependencies, derailing project progress.

   e. Misunderstandings between stakeholders, developers, and end-users – Differing expectations and unclear requirements lead to conflicts, rework, and a product that misses the mark.
2. Budget and Time Overruns: One common reason for IT project failure is budget and time overruns, often resulting from inaccurate forecasts and underestimated resource needs.
3. Lack of Skilled Resources: IT projects often fail due to a lack of skilled resources, as the shortage of qualified personnel hinders the ability to manage and execute complex tasks effectively.
4. Technological Challenges
   a. Unexpected technical issues: Unexpected technical issues can disrupt IT projects by introducing unforeseen complications that delay progress and require unplanned resource allocation.
   b. Integration problems: Integration problems often arise when new systems must interface with legacy infrastructure, leading to compatibility issues and increased project complexity.
   c. Evolving technologies can derail projects: Evolving technologies can derail projects by rendering chosen solutions obsolete or forcing mid-project shifts in tools, platforms, or standards.

In summary, IT project failures often stem from a combination of poor planning, resource limitations, technical challenges, and the inability to adapt to changing technologies and environments.

From small-scale computing to large-scale software development, engineers must contend with challenges such as machine errors, rapid technological evolution, team diversity, remote collaboration, and other complexities. Software engineering has introduced various solutions to address these issues, ranging from Model Integrated Computing (MIC) to Microsoft's Software Factories and the OMG's Model-Driven Architecture (MDA).

In this context, the Object Management Group (OMG) promotes the development of interoperable solutions, where interoperability refers to a system's ability to seamlessly interact with others, regardless of their internal implementation. These principles form the foundation of Model-Driven Engineering (MDE), which emphasizes abstraction, automation, and standardization to improve software development.

1.2 MDE Concepts

The main concepts related to Model Driven Engineering are: Models, Metamodels and transformations.

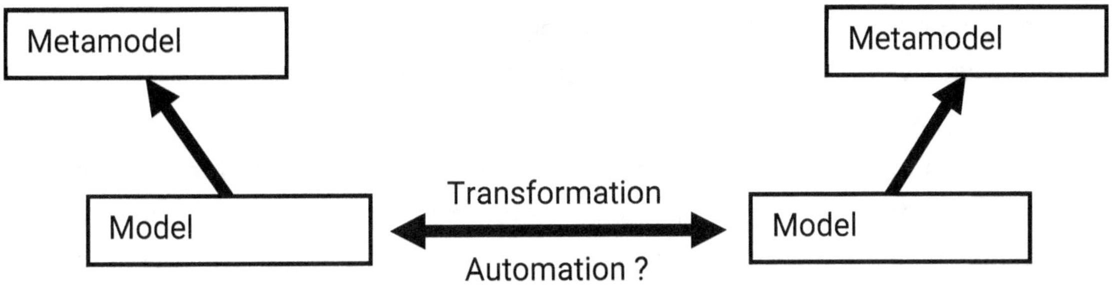

Figure 3 Main concepts of the MDE

1.2.1 The model

It can be defined as:

- A description of an existing system such as a house photo;
- A partial specification of a projected system such as house plan;
- A restricted set of the system information such as a student file;
- A subjective and simplified view of the system such a pictogram on a road sign.

Why model things? The answer is straightforward: modeling is essential. In the realm of system design and analysis, modeling serves as a foundational tool that enables us to simulate, analyze, and comprehend complex systems. Without models, we would lack the ability to predict system behavior, test scenarios virtually, or break down intricate systems into understandable components. Modeling provides the abstraction needed to manage complexity, optimize designs, and facilitate communication among stakeholders. Simply put, in engineering and software development, we model because we must—it is the bridge between conceptual ideas and functional systems.

1.2.1.1 Model types

Context models

Define the system's boundaries and relationships with external entities. Common examples include:

- Context Diagrams (showing system scope and external interfaces)
- Data Flow Diagrams (illustrating information flows between system components)

Interaction models

Focus on communication patterns between system components. Key representations are:

- Sequence Diagrams (temporal ordering of interactions)
- Use Case Modeling (user-system interactions and requirements)

Structural models

Represent the static architecture and organization of system components:

- Class Diagrams (object-oriented structure)
- Aggregation Diagrams (whole-part relationships)
- Generalization Diagrams (inheritance hierarchies)

Behavioral models

Capture dynamic aspects of system operation through:

- Event-Driven Modeling (system responses to events)
- Data-Driven Modeling (behavior triggered by data changes)

1.2.2 The Metamodel

The metamodel, is the descriptor of the model. It defines: How to create a model, and how to read it too. A model has to conform to his metamodel. Let's take two examples:
A sentence that describes an event is a model that represent the event itself – Its metamodel is the set of rules describing the spoken language.
The second example is the map, the map is a model that describe a terrain which is the system – Its metamodel is the map legend that indicates the meaning of colors, traits and measurements.

1.2.3 The Model Transformation

Transformations describe relation among models: A transformation takes one or many models as input, and gives one or more models in output. When the input models have the same metamodels as the output models, this transformation is called endogenous, otherwise, it is called exogenous.
All these notions define the OMG pyramid which is (from bottom to top);

1. The system (or the data) that is the reality and is unique.
2. The model that represents the system (called metadata) and is multiple.
3. The metamodel that describe the model.
4. The meta-metamodel that describe the metamodel, and has to be circular (sufficient to describe itself to avoid higher levels in the pyramid).

1.3 MDE Motivation

1.3.1 Permanent evolution of technologies

In computing, we utilize diverse technologies including modeling languages, database systems, platforms, operating systems, markup languages, file formats, and programming languages. These components may reside on the same machine or be distributed across networks.
To enable interoperability among these heterogeneous systems, various solutions have been developed:

- Low-level protocols: C sockets with TCP/UDP
- Distributed computing paradigms: RPC, CORBA, RMI, EJB
- Modern standards: Web services (SOAP/REST)

Middleware and message brokers facilitate communication between distributed systems, handling differences in platforms and languages. Similarly, software development requires paradigms that unify disparate tools and processes. Crucially, these solutions must ensure concurrent execution (collaborative functionality) while maintaining fault isolation—allowing components to fail independently without cascading disruptions.

1.3.2 Need to communicate distant elements

Model-Driven Engineering (MDE) addresses the critical challenge of interoperability among distributed system components—including applications, processes, threads, and resources—which often operate in heterogeneous environments. By providing standardized modeling abstractions and tool-agnostic frameworks, MDE enables consistent communication and collaboration across all project stakeholders (developers, architects, domain experts), ensuring seamless integration from design to deployment.

1.3.3 Separation of concerns

In software development, a fundamental principle is the separation of *data* from *algorithms*, which forms the foundation of object-oriented programming. This division safeguards data integrity by preventing unintended manipulation and creates a controlled environment for developers, enabling better error isolation and fault containment.

Building on this, **Model-Driven Engineering (MDE)** extends the paradigm further by decoupling *business logic* from *implementation specifics* and *platform dependencies*. This approach introduces:

- A **high-level abstract model** (platform-independent, focusing on business requirements),
- An **implementation model** (platform-specific, detailing technical execution),
- **Projection/transformation models** (automating the mapping between abstraction and implementation).

Additionally, cross-cutting concerns like *security policies*, *access privileges*, and *stakeholder-specific requirements* can be systematically integrated into these layers, ensuring holistic system design.

1.4 Relations in MDE

Between models, metamodels and systems, there are relations that must be respected:

Conformance means that all elements in the model must adhere to the definitions and constraints of the metamodel. This enables tool support for validation, editing, transformation, and code generation.

Representation means that the model captures the essential aspects of a system to understand, analyze, communicate, or automate its construction. A model must faithfully represent some real or imagined system from a specific viewpoint and for a specific purpose.

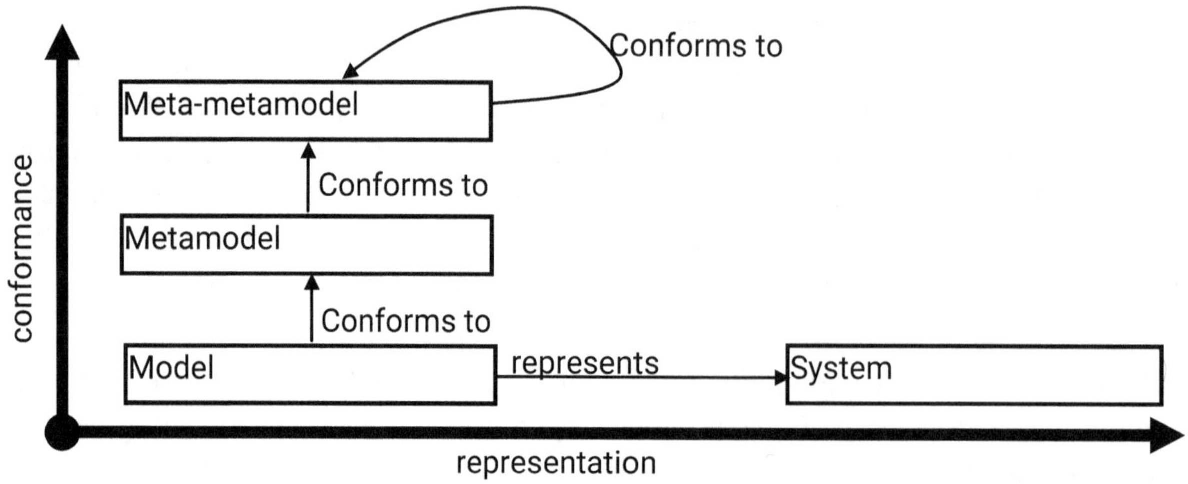

Figure 4 Relations among concepts in the MDE

1.5 The beginning – MDA

The Model Driven Architecture (MDA) is the MDE solution of OMG. This architecture separates the business logic from the implementation details. This separation is expressed using the OMG tools such as UML, OCL, MOF. The MDA solution is based on four model types: PIM, PSM, CIM and PDM models.

1.5.1 The Platform Independent Model

- It describes the business-oriented processing and is a design model;
- The PIM describes the system independently of any technical platform and any technology used to deploy the application;
- It represents system-specific business logic: The functioning of entities and services;
- This model is sustainable over time;
- The PIM consists of class diagrams with OCL constraints;
- The different levels of PIM specify the choices of persistence, transaction management and security.

1.5.2 The Platform Specific Model

- This model specifies the solution after projection on a technological platform.
- PSM specify the technical details related to the implementation for a platform: It depends on this platform;
- It is used to generate executable code for particular technical platforms;
- The PSM model describes how the system will use the platform. There are several PSM for a project over levels:
    1. The first level, resulting from the transformation of a PIM by adapting UML models to the specificities of the used platform.
    2. The other PSM levels are obtained by successive transformations taking into account the language (Java, CPP, PHP, etc.) and design choices.

3. The last level, or implementation PSM, describes, among other things, the program code, the table schemas, the libraries used and the deployment descriptors.

1.5.3 The Computational Independent Model

- This model describes the system specification from an external user's perspective.
- It describes the flows and the actions on the system;
- The CIM can be defined as a basic business or application domain analysis model;
- It is independent of any computer system or paradigm;
- This model Describes business activity concepts, know-how, processes, terminology and management rules (it is a very high-level model);
- CIM describes the situation in which the system is used and is modified only if knowledge or business needs change (it has a very long life, more than the PIM model);
- The requirements modeled in the CIM will be taken into account in constructions of PIMs and PSMs.

1.5.4 The Platform Deployment Model

- This model describes the deployment rules for a given technological platform. And describes a technical architecture (There may be several ones per project);
- The PDM contains information allowing transformation of conceptual models to a given platform;
- This model is platform specific;
- It is a transformation model to enable the transition from PIM to PSM;

1.5.5 The Y development cycle

The development cycle in MDA is a cascade of *Y* cycle parts. The PIM models are converted to PSM models according to the PDM specifications (See Figure 6 and Figure 5).

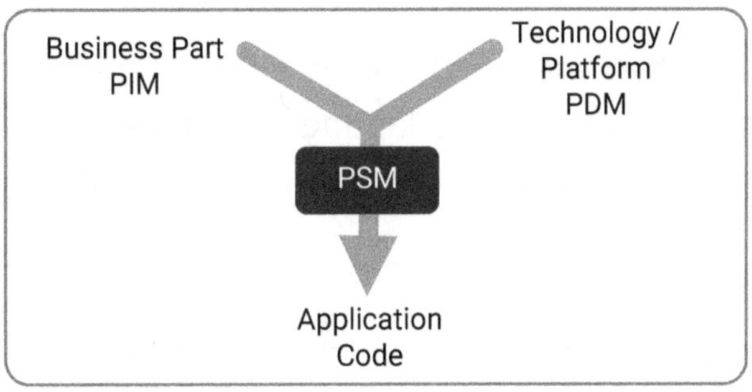

Figure 5 The MDA Y-development cycle

1.6 From MDA to MDE

To generalize the MDA concepts, we can extract 4 main concepts:

1.6.1 Capitalization (Reuse of items)

Reusing models or parts of models allows developers to rely on previously defined structures and behaviors, thus reducing redundancy and improving project efficiency. Reusability not only concerns the concrete parts of the project, but also encompasses ideas, solutions, and paradigms.

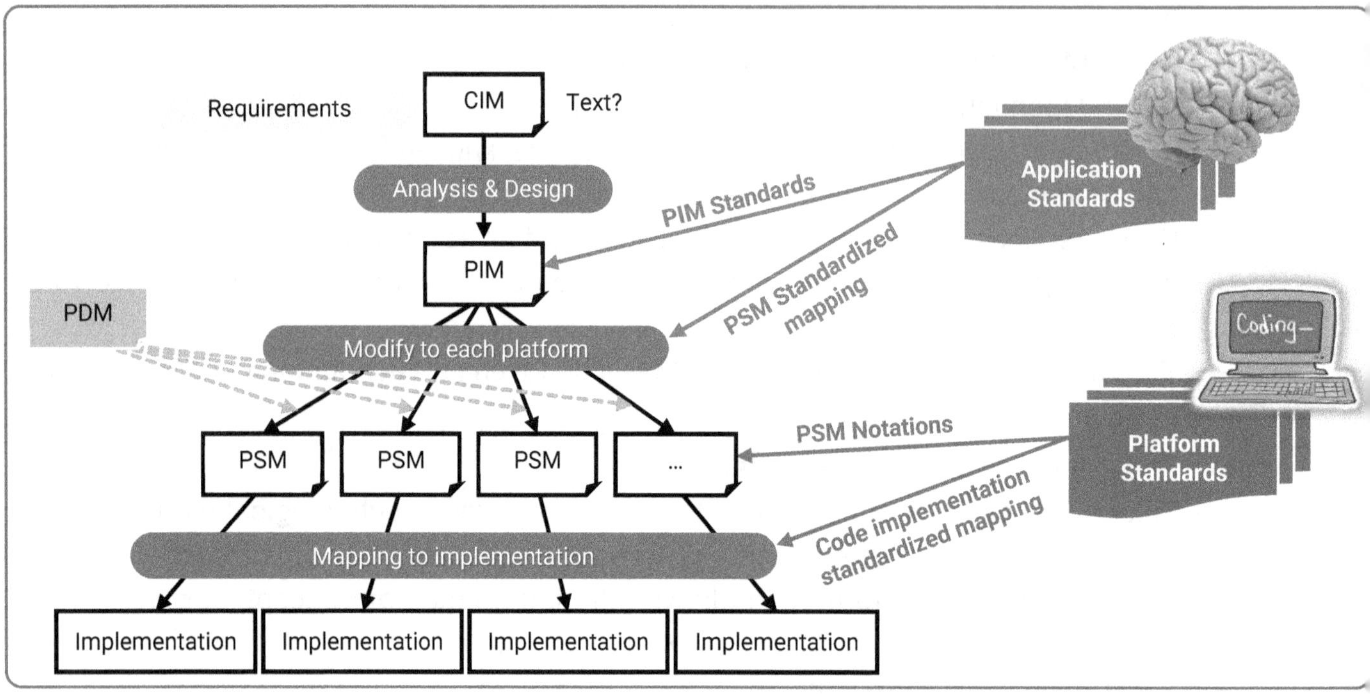

Figure 6 Mapping from CIM to Implementations in the MDA paradigm

This approach promotes the transition from creating isolated, one-off solutions to designing systems as assemblies of modular and reusable components, adaptable and integrable in various contexts and situations.

1.6.2 Abstraction

MDA enables the adaptation of business logic to specific application contexts, ensuring that core functionality remains relevant while adapting to different operational environments, and it facilitates system evolution by enabling integration or migration to new and emerging technologies.

1.6.3 Separation of concerns

This approach separates the business logic, which defines the system's core functionality, from the platform-specific implementation and other cross-functional concerns such as security and user interfaces.

These additional concerns are modeled independently and then integrated into the system via model transformations, ensuring modularity, flexibility, and simplified maintenance.

1.6.4 Modeling

Modeling should be productive enough to support automatic generation of source code tailored to a specific implementation technology, thereby reducing hand-coding efforts and speeding up the development process.

Chapter 2. Object Constraint Language

Object Constraint Language (OCL) is a formal language used to precisely and clearly describe the expressions, rules, and constraints of UML models. Unlike some programming languages, OCL is declarative, making it ideal for specifying invariants, preconditions, postconditions, and derived values within models. It improves the expressiveness of models by enabling the definition of business rules and validation logic that cannot be captured by diagrams alone.

2.1 Introductory example

To better understand OCL, let's start with an introductory example. Consider the following example of a banking system management application. The requirements are:

- Management of accounts, customers, and banks.
- The account balance is always positive.
- A customer can have multiple accounts.
- A customer can be a customer of multiple banks.
- A customer of a bank has at least one account in that bank and a holder of an account in a bank is a customer in that bank.
- A bank manages multiple accounts.
- A bank has multiple customers.

A solution to these requirements could be the following class diagram:

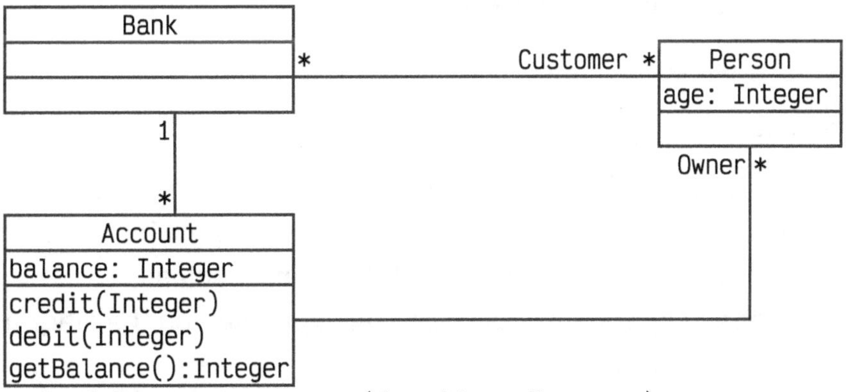

Now, considering the following instances (the object diagrams):

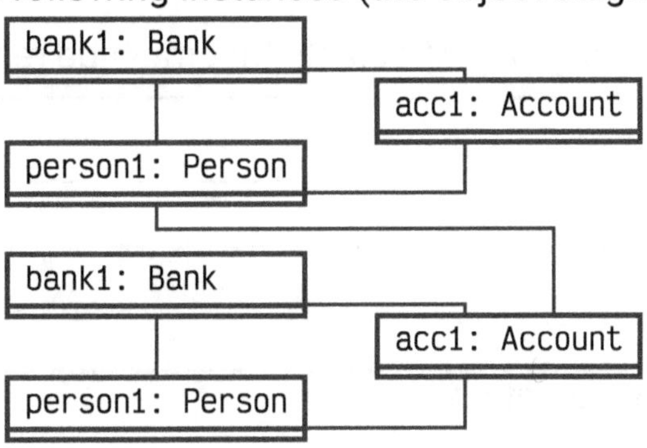

The above class diagram conforms to the model (Class Diagram), but it does not conform to the initial specifications, notably: A customer of a bank has at least one account in that bank and a holder of an account in a bank is a customer in that bank.
This anomaly can only be specified in the class diagram by notes because it does not concern the definition, but the instances which are the objects. Hence the interest in defining a language allowing the expression of these constraints on objects: OCL – Object Constraint Language.

2.2 OCL Constraints

OCL constraints are expressed at the Class definition level (Type definition), but the semantics are defined at the object level.

2.3 What does OCL allow to express?

Constraints on the state of an object or a set of objects, including:

- **Invariants** which must be respected at all times.
- Pre- and post-conditions for an operation:
  - **Pre-condition**: must be checked before execution.
  - **Post-condition**: must be checked after execution.

Do not confuse the constraints to be respected with the method code. Constraints are logical expressions that evaluate to true or false, and not machine instructions involving modification of the state of registers and memories.

2.3.1 The context

```
context Account
inv: balance > 0
context Account::debit(sum_ : Integer)
pre: sum_ > 0
post: balance = balance@pre - sum_
context Account
inv: bank.customer -> includes (owner)
```

An OCL expression is defined in a context, which is an element of the model (class or operation) introduced by the reserved word **context** accompanying the diagram.
The expression then applies to all instances of this **context** class.
The constraint is written separately or can also be expressed on the diagram: By pointing to it with the expression put between { } in a note.

2.3.2 The invariants

Express a constraint on an object or group of objects that must be respected at all times:

```
inv: <logical_expression>
```

2.3.3 Pre- and Post-condition

```
pre: <logical_expression>
post: <logical_expression>
```

result is the value returned by the operation.

<attribute_name>@pre is the value of the attribute **<attribute_name>** before calling the operation.

2.3.4 Example of use :

```
context Account::getBalance():Integer
post: result = balance
context Account::debit(sum_ : Integer)
pre: sum_ > 0
post: balance = balance@pre - sum_
```

Explanation: The amount to be debited must be positive for the call of the operation to be valid.

After the execution of the operation, the balance attribute must have for value its value before the call from which was subtracted the *sum_ passed* in parameter.

2.4 Access to Objects

In an OCL constraint associated with an object, we can:

1. Access the internal state of this object (its attributes): to access the attributes or parameters of an operation, we use their name directly
2. Navigate in the diagram: transitive access to all the objects (and their state) with which it is related. To access the objects with associations, we can use three methods:
    a. The name of the associated class (with the first letter in lowercase)
    b. The name of the association if it is named.
    c. The name of the association role on the side of the class to which it is navigated if it is named.

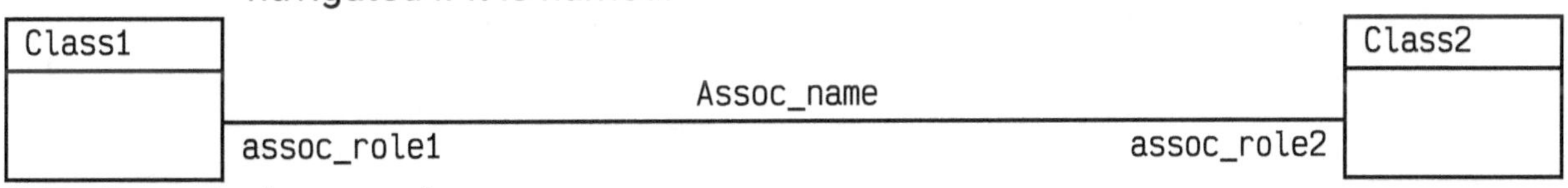

2.5 Practical examples

Now we will extend our class diagram as follows

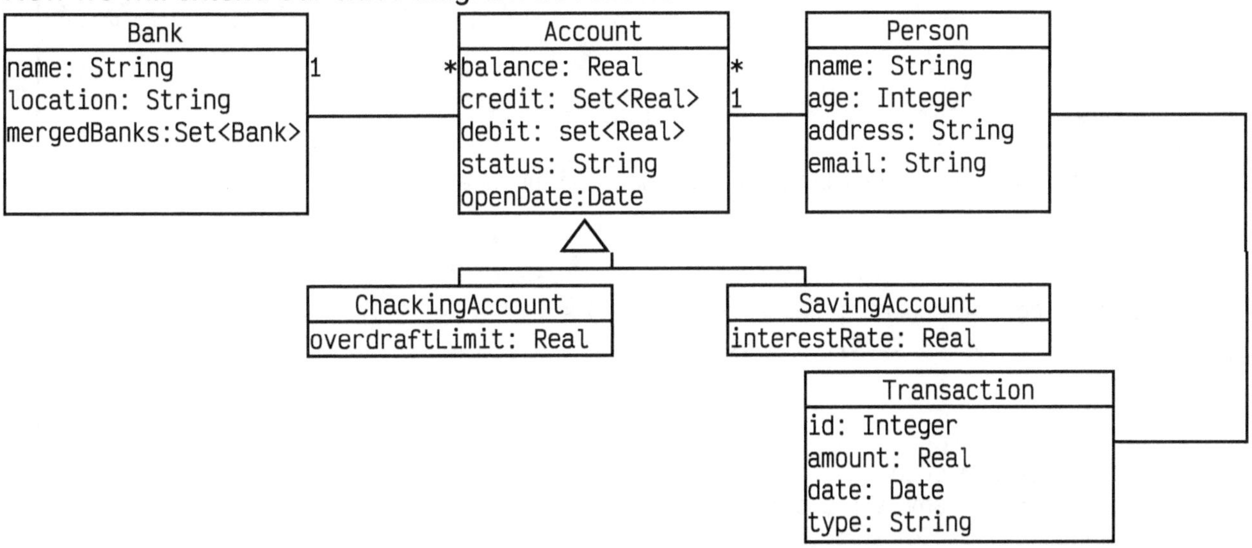

2.5.1 Basic vocabulary explanation

inv – Specifies an invariant that must always be true for all instances of the class.
pre – Defines a precondition that must hold before an operation executes.
post – Defines a postcondition that must hold after an operation executes.
def – Creates a derived attribute or helper operation.
context - Specifies which class or operation the constraints apply to.
self - Refers to the current instance being constrained.

2.5.2 Collection operations explanation

select – Filters a collection to only include elements satisfying a condition
reject – Filters a collection to exclude elements satisfying a condition
collect – Transforms each element in a collection
sortedBy – Orders a collection based on specified attributes
any – Returns any element from a collection that satisfies a condition
exists – True if at least one element satisfies the condition
forAll – True if all elements satisfy the condition
one – True if exactly one element satisfies the condition
isUnique – True if all elements have unique values for the specified property

2.5.3 Constraint samples

2.5.3.1 Bank Class Constraints

```
context Bank
-- This is a comment !
-- Select only active accounts (using 'select')
inv activeAccounts:
    self.accounts->select(a | a.status = 'Active')->notEmpty()
-- Explanation: "Filters accounts to only those with Active status and verifies at
              least one exists"

-- Reject frozen accounts (using 'reject')
inv noFrozenAccounts:
    self.accounts->reject(a | a.status = 'Frozen')->size() = self.accounts->size()
    Explanation: "Removes any frozen accounts from consideration and compares
              collection sizes"

-- Collect all customer names (using 'collect')
inv uniqueCustomers:
    self.accounts.owner->collect(p | p.name)->isUnique()
-- Explanation: "Gathers all owner names and verifies they are distinct"

-- Sorted list of accounts by open date (using 'sortedBy')
def: chronologicalAccounts: Sequence(Account) =
    self.accounts->sortedBy(openDate)
-- Explanation: "Creates an ordered sequence of accounts from oldest to newest"

-- Check if any account has exactly zero balance (using 'any')
inv hasZeroBalanceAccount:
    self.accounts->any(a | a.balance = 0)->notEmpty()
-- Explanation: "Verifies existence of at least one account with zero balance"
```

2.5.3.2 Account Class Constraints

```
context Account
-- Verify all transactions are valid (using 'forAll')
inv validTransactions:
    self.transactions->forAll(t | t.amount > 0 and t.date <= Date.now())
-- Explanation: "Ensures every transaction has positive amount and isn't future-
dated"

-- Exactly one owner must exist (using 'one')
inv singleOwner:
    self.owner->one()
-- Explanation: "Account must have exactly one owner"

-- Unique transaction IDs (using 'isUnique')
inv uniqueTransactionIds:
    self.transactions->isUnique(id)
-- Explanation: "All transaction IDs must be unique within this account"

-- Complex boolean expression (using 'xor', 'implies')
inv validStatusCombination:
    (self.isActive xor self.isClosed) and
    (self.balance < 0 implies self.oclIsTypeOf(CheckingAccount))
-- Explanation: "Account can't be both active/closed, and only checking accounts
                 can be overdrawn"
```

2.5.3.3 Person Class Constraints

```
context Person
-- Name must have first and last parts (using 'substring', 'includes')
inv fullName:
    self.name.substring(1, self.name.size()).includes(' ') and
    self.name.size() >= 5
-- Explanation: "Name must contain space and be at least 5 characters"

-- Address validation (using 'concat', 'size')
inv validAddress:
    self.address.concat(' ', self.city).size() <= 100
-- Explanation: "Combined address fields shouldn't exceed 100 characters"

-- Age-specific rules (using 'if-then-else')
def: accountLimit: Integer =
    if self.age < 18 then 1 else 10 endif
-- Explanation: "Minors limited to 1 account, adults can have up to 10"

-- Email format check (using 'oclIsUndefined')
inv validEmail:
    not self.email.oclIsUndefined() implies
    self.email.includes('@') and
    self.email.substring(self.email.size()-4).includes('.')
-- Explanation: "If email exists, it must contain @ and have a domain suffix"
```

2.5.3.4 Type Operations

```
context Account
-- Type-specific constraints (using 'oclIsTypeOf', 'oclAsType')
inv savingAccountRules:
    self.oclIsTypeOf(SavingAccount) implies
    self.oclAsType(SavingAccount).interestRate > 0
-- Explanation: "Savings accounts must have positive interest rate"
-- State verification (using 'oclInState')
inv activeAccountOperations:
    self.oclInState('Active') implies self.transactions->notEmpty()
-- Explanation: "Active accounts must have at least one transaction"
-- New account check (using 'oclIsNew')
context Account::open()
post:
    self.oclIsNew() and self.openDate = Date.now()
-- Explanation: "Newly opened accounts get current date timestamp"
```

2.5.3.5 Numeric Operations

```
context Account
-- Balance formatting (using 'floor', 'abs')
def: displayBalance: String =
    if self.balance < 0
    then '-$' + self.balance.abs().floor().toString()
    else '$' + self.balance.floor().toString()
    endif
-- Explanation: "Formats balance as currency with proper negative handling"
-- Transaction limits (using 'sum')
inv dailyDepositLimit:
    self.transactions->select(t | t.date = Date.today() and t.amount > 0)
       ->sum(amount) <= 10000
-- Explanation: "Total daily deposits cannot exceed $10,000"
-- Overdraft protection (using 'max')
inv overdraftProtection:
    self.balance >= -self.overdraftLimit.max(1000)
-- Explanation: "Negative balance cannot exceed overdraft limit (minimum $1000)"
```

2.5.3.6 Collection Operations

```
context Bank
-- Account inclusion/exclusion (using 'includes', 'excludes', 'includingAll')
inv premiumAccounts:
    self.accounts->includes(self.premiumAccount) or
    self.accounts->excluding(self.premiumAccount)->size() < self.accounts->size()
-- Explanation: "Verifies premium account is either included or collection size
                 changes when excluded"
-- Merged accounts (using 'includingAll')
def: allManagedAccounts: Set(Account) =
    self.accounts->includingAll(self.affiliates.accounts)
-- Explanation: "Combines all accounts from bank and its affiliates"
-- Transaction verification (using 'exists')
inv largeTransactionCheck:
    self.accounts.transactions->exists(amount > 100000)
-- Explanation: "Flags if any transaction exceeds $100,000"
```

2.6 Writing guidelines

2.6.1 Avoid complex navigations

Overly long or deeply nested navigation chains in OCL constraints reduce readability, increase the risk of null references, and make constraints harder to maintain and debug. For example, instead of writing:

```
self.department.company.division.region.country
```

Try to refactor the model or add associations to simplify this chain.

2.6.2 Choose the appropriate context

Defining constraints in the most relevant context (typically the class that owns or is most directly related to the constraint logic) ensures clarity, reduces unnecessary navigation, and improves model modularity. For example, If you want to express a constraint that every student must be enrolled in at least one course, place the constraint in the Student context:

```
context Student inv: self.courses->notEmpty()
```

2.6.3 Avoid using allInstances()

Using **allInstances()** can lead to performance issues and is discouraged because it may not behave consistently across tools and platforms, especially in large models or when not all instances are explicitly created. For example, instead of:

```
Person.allInstances()->select(p | p.age > 18)
```

Prefer a model structure that allows navigating from a known instance, such as:

```
self.department.employees->select(e | e.age > 18)
```

2.6.4 Optimize the use of and in constraints

While combining multiple conditions with and is common, grouping logically related expressions or splitting them into separate invariants can improve readability and maintainability. For example, instead of:

```
context Order
inv: self.total > 0 and self.status = 'Confirmed' and self.customer->notEmpty()
```

You can split into two invariants:

```
inv PositiveTotal: self.total > 0 and self.status = 'Confirmed'
inv HasCustomer: self.customer->notEmpty()
```

2.6.5 Work with collections (even for attributes)

Treating attributes as collections (e.g., using **->asSet()** or **->asSequence()**) allows the use of OCL's powerful collection operations for filtering, mapping, or checking conditions. For example, to check if any of a person's email addresses end with *".edu"*:

```
self.emailAddresses->exists(e | e.endsWith('.edu'))
```

2.6.6 Prefer using role names

Using role names instead of raw association ends clarifies the semantics of the model, reflects design intent more clearly, and makes constraints easier to understand. For example, Instead of self.worksFor, if the role name is employer, write:

```
self.employer->notEmpty()
```

2.7 Collections

In OCL, the type of collection resulting from navigation depends on the structure of the model:

- A single association navigation yields a **Set**;
- Combined or repeated navigations produce a **Bag**;
- Navigating over associations marked as **{ordered}** returns an **OrderedSet**.

These collection types—defined in the OCL Standard Library—play a crucial role in forming correct and meaningful OCL expressions.

OCL defines an abstract supertype called **Collection**, from which the concrete collection types **Set**, **Sequence**, and **Bag** are derived. Each type offers a variety of predefined operations that allow modelers to query and manipulate collections in a declarative and side-effect-free way. As OCL is strictly an expression language, all collection operations are pure queries (**isQuery** is always **true**); they do not modify the original collection but instead return a new one as the result of the operation.

The semantics of each collection type are as follows:

- **Set** represents a mathematical set: it contains no duplicate elements and has no defined order.
- **Bag** is an unordered collection that **may contain duplicates**, meaning the same element can appear multiple times.
- **Sequence** is similar to a Bag but with a defined **order** of elements. Note that both **Set** and **Bag** are unordered, while only **Sequence** preserves the order of its elements.

2.7.1 Collection Literals

Sets, **Sequences**, and **Bags** can be specified by a **literal** in OCL. Curly brackets surround the elements of the collection, elements in the collection are written within, separated by commas. The type of the collection is written before the curly brackets:

1. A set

```
Set { 1 , 88, 5, 2 }
Set { 'strawberry', 'apple', 'orange' }
```

2. A Sequence:

```
Sequence { 45, 3, 3, 2, 1 }
Sequence { 'ape', 'nut' }
```

3. A bag:

```
Bag {1, 3, 4, 3, 5 }
```

Because of the usefulness of a Sequence of consecutive Integers, there is a separate literal to create them. The elements inside the curly brackets can be replaced by an interval specification, which consists of two expressions of type Integer, **Int-expr1** and **Int-expr2**, separated by '..'. This denotes all the Integers between the values of Int-expr1 and Int-expr2, including the values of Int-expr1 and Int-expr2 themselves:

```
Sequence{ 1..(6 + 4) }
Sequence{ 1..10 }
-- are both identical to
Sequence{ 1, 2, 3, 4, 5, 6, 7, 8, 9, 10 }
```

Collections can be specified by a literal, as described above. The only other way to get a collection is by navigation. To be more precise, the only way to get a **Set**, **OrderedSet**, **Sequence**, or **Bag** is:

1. A literal, this will result in a **Set**, **OrderedSet**, **Sequence**, or **Bag**:

```
Set {2 , 4, 1 , 5 , 7 , 13, 11, 17 }
OrderedSet {1 , 2, 3 , 5 , 7 , 11, 13, 17 }
Sequence {1 , 2, 3 , 5 , 7 , 11, 13, 17 }
Bag {1, 2, 3, 2, 1}
```

2. A navigation starting from a single object can result in a collection:

```
context Company inv:
self.employee
```

3. Operations on collections may result in new collections:

```
collection1->union(collection2)
```

Chapter 3. Metamodeling with MOF

Metamodeling is the meta-level of modeling. The prefix "meta" comes from the Greek *μετά* (meta), meaning after, beyond, or with. It conveys a range of ideas including reflection, transformation, succession, and the notion of going beyond or above. In various contexts, "meta" implies depth (as in metadata or metalanguage), hierarchy (as in a meta-review), or abstraction.

In scientific and technical disciplines, "meta" is frequently used to indicate self-reference or to denote a higher level of abstraction—that is, a system used to describe or structure other systems. Some common examples include:

- Metalanguage: a language used to describe other languages;
- Metabook: a book about another book;
- Metadocumentation: documentation about documentation;
- Metadata: data that describes other data.

In the field of metamodeling, this prefix signifies that a metamodel is a specification that defines the structure, semantics, and constraints of other models.

3.1 Definitions

A **model** is a simplified representation of a system, while a **metamodel** is a model that defines the structure and rules for creating such models—it describes how models themselves are constructed. To illustrate this with a concrete example:

- The **system** is a running thread on a computer.
- The **model** is the program written in a specific programming language, whose execution produces the thread.
- The **metamodel** is the grammar of the programming language, typically described using **Extended Backus-Naur Form (eBNF)**.
- In this context, the **eBNF rules** serve as the **meta-metamodel**, as they define the valid syntax and structure of programs (i.e., models) in that language.
- This example highlights the core idea of metamodeling: just as a program models a computational behavior, the grammar (metamodel) defines how valid programs (models) are formed.

3.2 The MDE metamodeling concept hierarchy and relations

The diagram of **Error! Reference source not found.** illustrates the four-layer metamodeling architecture, commonly used to explain the levels of abstraction in model-driven engineering.

At the base (M0), we find the actual system, represented by a model at level M1. This model conforms to a metamodel (M2), which defines the structure and rules that valid models must follow. The metamodel itself is defined using a meta-metamodel at level M3, which provides the fundamental constructs necessary to describe metamodels. To avoid becoming an infinite process, level M3 is often cyclical, closed, or self-defining, in the sense that the meta-metamodel is itself the meta-meta-metamodel.

The model, which can be multiple, represents its system, which can only be unique. Representativeness is then a relationship between the model and its system, and is also a relationship between each metamodel and its metamodeling language—a metamodeling language is the set of all conceivable conforming models—in a horizontal relationship.

Each model must, in turn, conform to its metamodel in a vertical relationship.

Membership, on the other hand, is a diagonal relationship expressed by the symbol ε indicating the relationships between the model and the set of all conforming models of the same metamodel.

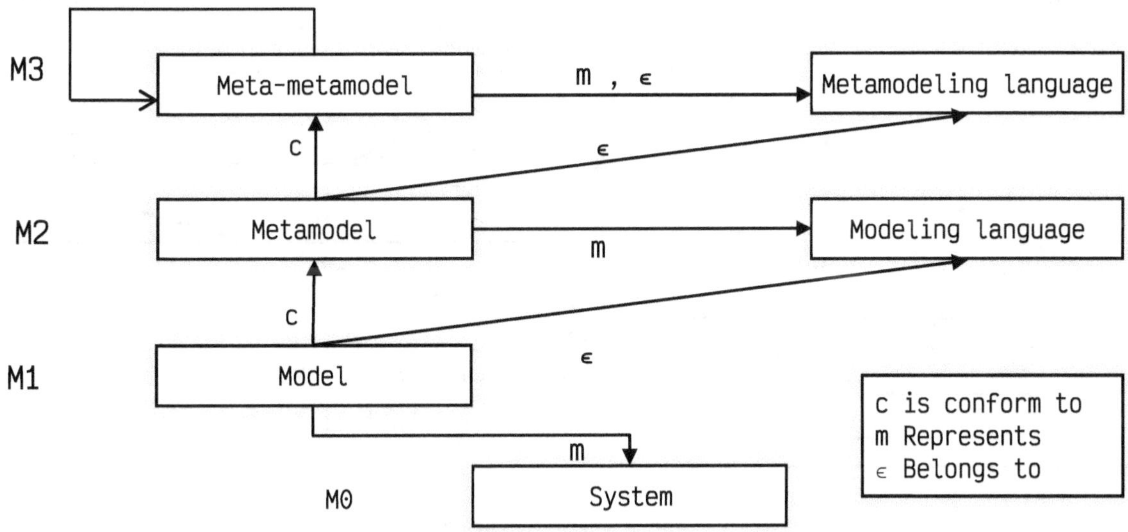

Figure 7 Metamodeling concepts in MDE

3.3 Metamodeling example

Let's take a simple example: a class diagram for which we want to define the metamodel. The definition of a metamodel could be summarized as a model description in a textual or graphical language. Consider the following model:

(M) A UML package containing a Customer class with a name attribute.

The description of such a model could be as follows:

(MM) A class containing attributes.

This description (MM) is a metamodel of (M). This metamodeling can be represented graphically by Figure 8.
At a higher level, to metamodel the previous metamodel, we can say:
(MMM) Classes have associations between them, their relationships are oriented (source to target). This meta-metamodel can be represented graphically by Figure 10.
The top level, on the other hand, is identical to the current level:
(MMM) Classes have associations with each other, their relationships are directed (source to target). This level is then **circular** (capable of defining itself) (Summarized in Figure 9).

3.4 Meta-Object Facility (MOF)

Meta-Object Facility (MOF) is a standard developed by the Object Management Group (OMG) to provide a platform-independent framework for defining, manipulating, and integrating metamodels. MOF serves as the basis for model-driven engineering (MDE) by enabling the creation of metamodels, which define the structure and semantics of models used in software development.
There are no specific levels defined in MOF; rather, it provides a paradigm for defining metamodels for models. Moving up a level, the same paradigm is used to define metamodels (which are, at this level, meta-metamodels) for models (which are, at this level, metamodels).

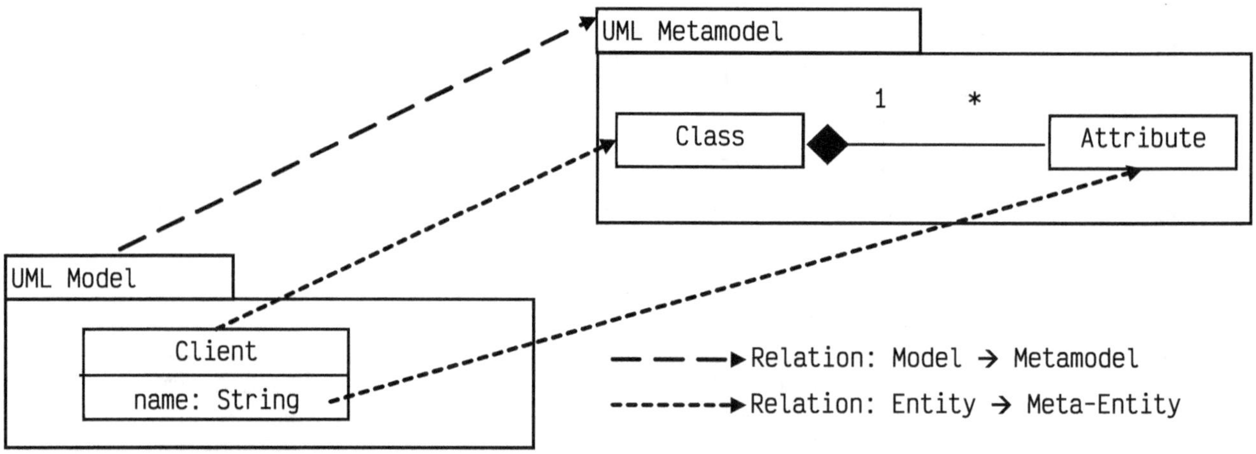

Figure 8 Graphic notation of creating metamodel of a simple class

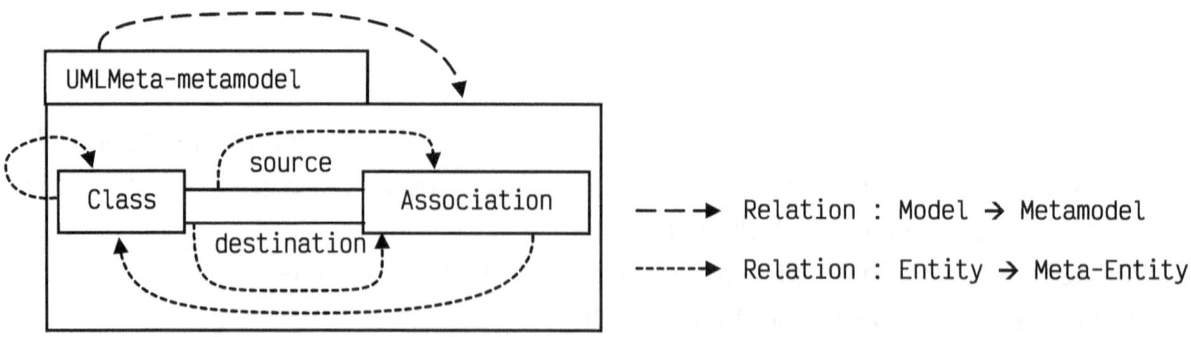

Figure 9 Meta-Circular Meta-Model example

MOF is defined as:

- **Meta-circular Meta-metamodel**, A meta-metamodel is said to be *meta-circular* when it is capable of defining itself using its own constructs—this property is known as **reflection**, which allows a model to be **self-describing** [OMG].
- Only a limited set of concepts—about twenty—is needed to define the **M2 metamodel layer**. Among these, the most essential are:
    - **Class** (defining attributes and optionally operations, depending on the MOF level used[1])
    - **Association** (defining relationships between classes)
    - **References** (typed links between model elements)
    - **Package** (used to group related elements and organize the model)

These core elements form the foundation for building expressive and coherent metamodels.

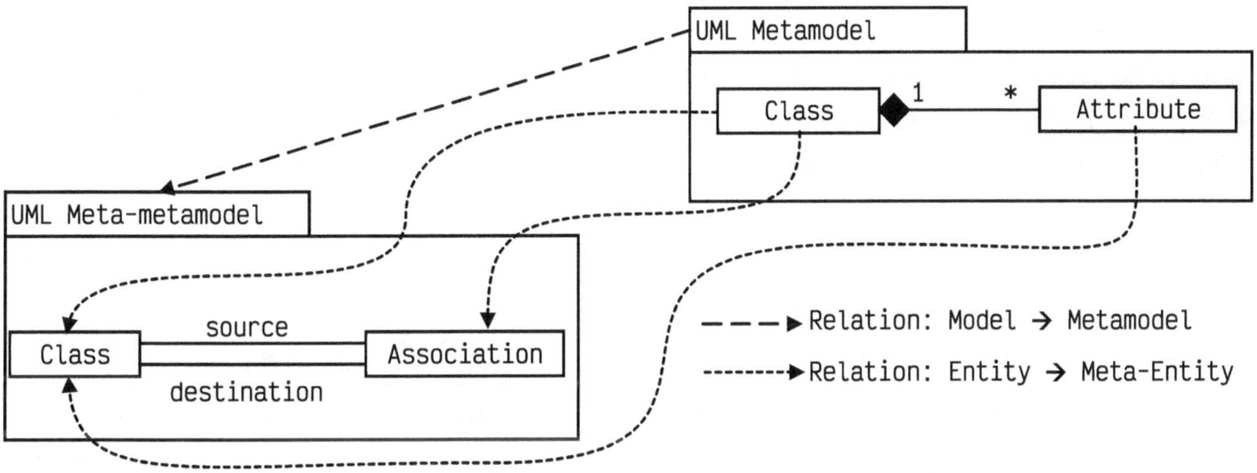

Figure 10 Graphic Notation of creating meta-metamodel

3.5 The metamodeling paradigm

3.5.1 Metamodel Definition

In Model-Driven Engineering (MDE), a modeling **language** (like UML, SysML, BPMN, etc.) is defined by its **metamodel**: The **metamodel** specifies the abstract syntax (the structure and rules) of the language.

[1] "Methods" might be omitted from the Class concept if you're strictly referencing **EMOF**, as EMOF doesn't define behavior (methods), only structure (attributes and references). CMOF, however, does support behavioral elements.

3.5.2 Element Representation

A metamodel defines the types of elements and their relationships that can appear in valid models of a language: A **metamodel defines the abstract structure** of models: what kinds of elements can exist (e.g., classes, attributes, associations) and how they relate.

3.5.3 Entities and Meta-entities

A **model** is composed of elements that are **entities** defined in the metamodel by **meta-entities**.

For example, a Person class in a model is an entity of the Class meta-entity in the metamodel.

3.5.4 Graphical Notation

MOF itself does not define a graphical syntax. However, metamodels defined using MOF are often represented graphically using UML class diagrams, and constraints are expressed with OCL. So, Metamodels defined in MOF are typically represented using UML class diagrams and constrained with OCL.

3.5.5 Abstract Syntax

MOF defines the abstract syntax for metamodels but does not define a concrete (textual or graphical) syntax for models or metamodels. Concrete syntaxes (like graphical editors or textual DSLs) are defined separately or through tooling (e.g., GMF, Xtext).

3.6 MOF Compliance

There are two versions of MOF, each tailored to specific use cases: EMOF (Essential MOF) and CMOF (Complete MOF). Let's break them down:

Feature	**EMOF (Essential MOF)**	**CMOF (Complete MOF)**
Purpose	Lightweight core suitable for most modeling needs.	Full-featured, includes all MOF capabilities.
Complexity	Simplified, minimal subset.	More complex and powerful.
Compatibility	Designed for easy mapping to XML, XMI, and tools like Eclipse EMF.	Matches closely with UML metamodels.
Support in Tools	Widely supported (e.g., Eclipse EMF, ATL, QVT).	Less widely supported due to complexity.
Key Features Omitted	No multiple inheritance, no package merge, fewer reflection capabilities.	Supports all MOF features including package merge, more advanced reflection.
Typical Use Cases	Lightweight metamodels, tool integration, transformations.	Full UML metamodels, complex modeling frameworks.
Tool support	Widely supported in model-driven tools like Eclipse EMF, ATL, Acceleo, QVT, etc ; Integrated easily with Ecore, making it a de facto standard in many open-source tools.	Supported primarily in OMG-compliant tools like MagicDraw, Enterprise Architect, or tools targeting full UML support ; Harder to implement in tooling due to its complex features like package merge.
	In practice: If you're building DSLs or doing model transformation with tools like EMF, ATL, or Xtext, you use EMOF.	
Use Case Focus	Designed for creating Domain-Specific Languages (DSLs) and simple metamodels;	Geared toward defining the full UML metamodel or other complex standards;

	Used for interoperability (e.g., exporting to XMI, transforming models).	Used when you need to be 100% UML-compliant or need features like multiple inheritance and package merge.
	Use EMOF for practical development, fast prototyping, and transformations. Use CMOF if you're defining or working with standardized metamodels like UML itself.	
Complexity and Learning Curve	EMOF is simpler and easier to understand; That's why educational tools and most tutorials focus on EMOF or Ecore.	CMOF is more complex, and using it often means dealing with full UML infrastructure, which can be overwhelming for simple modeling needs.
Model Interchange and Portability	EMOF is XMI-friendly, making it easier to serialize and exchange models between tools.	CMOF has incompatibilities with XMI, making model interchange more difficult without specific tool support.

Table 1 MOF Compliance Table

3.6.1 Core Concepts Used in MOF (especially CMOF)

Concept	Description
Class	Describes a type of object with structural features (attributes, references).
Attribute	A property of a class, typed and potentially multi-valued.
Reference	A unidirectional association from one class to another.
Association	A bidirectional relationship between two or more classes.
Property	A generalization of both attributes and references; defines a structural feature.
Operation	Defines behavior (like a method) on a class — used in CMOF but not EMOF.
Parameter	Used in operations to define input/output parameters.
Multiplicity	Specifies cardinality of attributes or references (e.g., 0..1, 1..*, etc.).
Generalization	Models inheritance between classes.
Enumeration	A predefined set of literals. Useful for value constraints.
DataType	A simple type that cannot have identity (e.g., Integer, String).
PrimitiveType	A predefined DataType like Integer, Boolean, etc.
Constraint	A condition or rule (often expressed in OCL) that must hold true.
Package	A namespace for grouping classes and other model elements.
ModelElement	The abstract root for all elements in a metamodel.
Comment	Allows annotations in models.

Table 2 MOF Concepts

3.6.2 Complete List of EMOF Concepts

EMOF Concept	Description
Class	Defines a type of model element with structural features (attributes, references).
Property	A structural feature of a class; includes both attributes and references.
Attribute	A property typed with a primitive or data type; holds values (e.g., strings, ints).
Reference	A property pointing to another class (typed link); may be containment or non-containment.
Multiplicity	Defined on properties to indicate cardinality (e.g., 0..1, 1..*, etc.).
DataType	A simple, non-identified type for defining attribute values (e.g., Date, URI).
Enumeration	A user-defined data type with a fixed set of named literals.
EnumerationLiteral	An element of an enumeration representing a constant value.
PrimitiveType	A built-in data type such as Integer, Boolean, String, and Real.
Package	A namespace that groups related classes and data types.

Model	Represents the root container of a model (used implicitly in many tools).
Comment	Provides textual annotations for documentation or notes.
Tag	Used to attach arbitrary metadata to model elements (as key-value pairs).
TypedElement	A common superclass of all elements that have a type (e.g., attributes, references).
NamedElement	A superclass for elements that have a name (e.g., classes, properties, packages).

Table 3 EMOF Concepts

3.7 Metamodel, model and metamodel instance

After the announced definitions, we must distinguish between three concepts related to this topic, which are the model, the metamodel and the instance of the metamodel which is the model of the model. Let's detail this with an example:

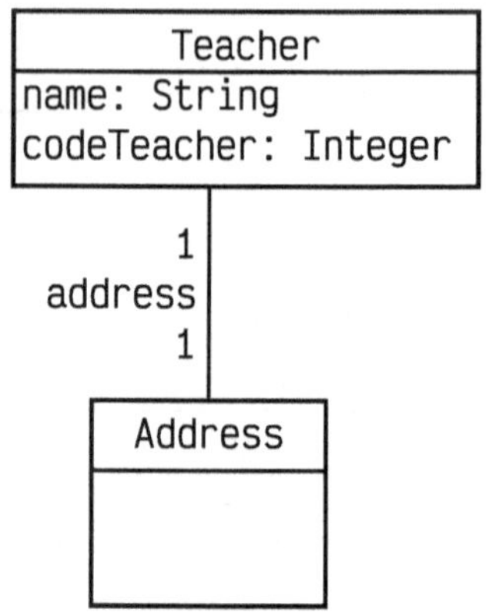

The opposite class diagram is a model representing a given system.
The metamodel for this model is a subset of the UML metamodel represented in Figure 11
When we instantiate the metamodel following the data of our model, we obtain another diagram which is not the model, nor the metamodel, but it is the model of our model (Figure 12).

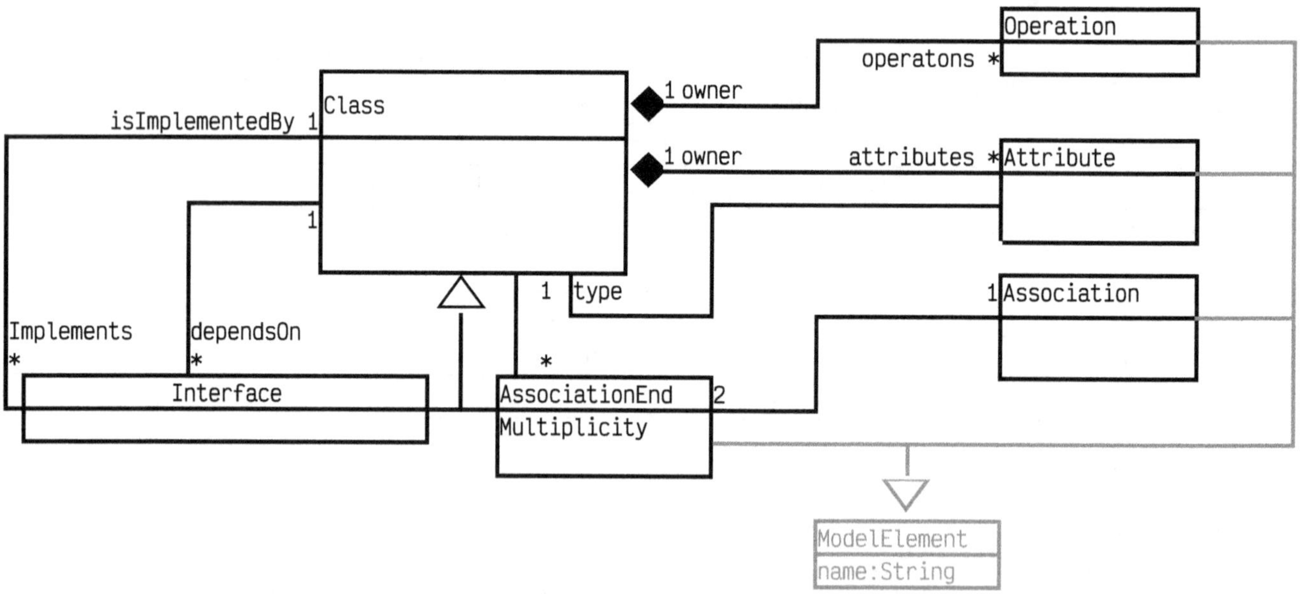

Figure 11 Partial UML metamodel

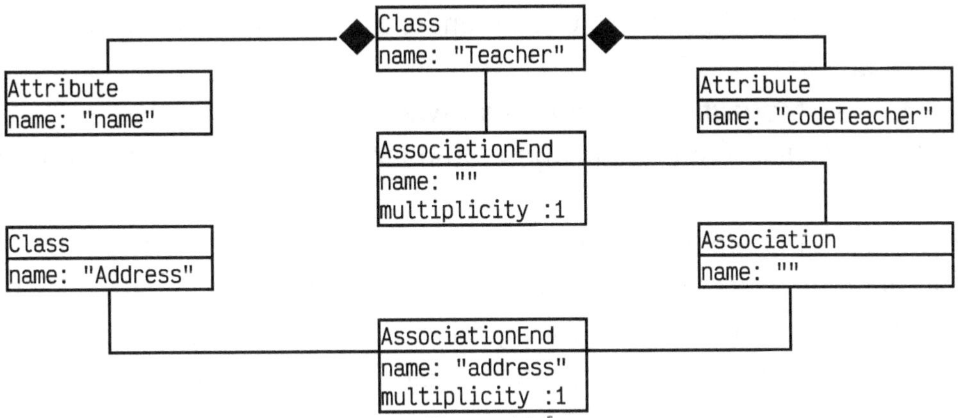

Figure 12 [
Figure 11–Metamodel] instance for the given model in section 3.7

3.8 Related concepts

The Meta-Object Facility (MOF), defined by the Object Management Group (OMG), is a meta-modeling architecture and standard for defining the structure, semantics, and constraints of modeling languages (such as UML).

MOF forms the basis for defining metamodels and is at the heart of the Model-Driven Architecture (MDA) framework. However, for MOF to be effective and provide comprehensive metamodel specifications, it requires other OMG tools, which we will cite below:

3.8.1 Xmi

In model-driven engineering, XML Metadata Interchange, abbreviated as XMI, is a standard created by the Object Management Group (OMG) for the exchange of UML metadata information based on XML. XMI is a serialization process[2] for MOF objects allowing objects to be described in XML format. This standard has been adopted by **ISO** and **IEC** under the number **ISO/IEC 19503**.

XML Metadata Interchange (XMI) is an OMG standard for exchanging metadata via the Extensible Markup Language (XML). It can be used for all metadata whose metamodel can be expressed in Meta-Object Facility (MOF). The most common use of XMI is the exchange of UML models, although it can also be used for the serialization of models from other languages (Or other metamodels.

So, the XMI is a bridge between two industry standards:

- **XML** – eXtensible Markup Language, which is a W3C standard;

[2] XMI is a serialization tool, meaning it allows you to transform a non-linear representation (such as an image, a graphic illustration, or multidimensional data) into a sequence of symbols (such as text).
In computing, it is the encoding of information as a sequence of smaller pieces of information, for example, storage (persistence) or transmission over a network (proxy, RPC, etc.). The reciprocal activity of decoding this sequence to create an exact copy of the original information is called deserialization (or unmarshalling). The term marshalling (mobilization, channeling, organization) is often used synonymously, as is the term linearization.

- **MOF** – Meta-Object Facility, an OMG standard for defining metamodels.

XMI is used in many other OMG standards such as:

- **UML** – Unified Modeling Language, a software modeling standard;
- **UMLDI** – UML Diagram Interchange – standard for graphical representation related to UML;
- **SysML** – Systems Modeling Language, a systems modeling standard.

These models, inheriting from the MOF metamodel, automatically benefit from the features of XMI to be represented with XML. The integration of these standards with XMI allows tools for developers of distributed systems to share their models and other metadata.

3.8.2 Moffol

This specification separates out those aspects of MOF related to communicating with and managing the "facilities" responsible for providing the capabilities covered by the other MOF specifications. These facilities may be at many different levels, from a modeling tool to a full multi-user, multi-model repository. The scope includes:

- Locating and connecting to facilities;
- Object lifecycle operations (e.g., creation and deletion); and
- Operational aspects (e.g., transactions).

3.8.3 Mofvd

During a system's evolution it will go through a number of iterations, driven by changes to a model at some level. The model for an existing deployed system is a valuable asset for understanding that system and making minor changes for bug fixes, etc. So it is important to preserve it when making broader changes for new functionality. The problem being addressed by this specification is to manage the co-existence of multiple versions of such metadata in a Meta Object Facility and their inclusion in different configurations (for example, a specific version of a Platform Independent Model (PIM), the corresponding version of the derived Platform Specific Model (PSM), and the corresponding version of the generated system).

A major problem related to the presence of multiple versions is to determine the correct one to use in response to a client request such as obtaining all instances of Package (it would not generally be useful to return many different versions of the same package), or even accessing the Features of a Class (again it would not be useful to return all Features the class has ever had, especially when some have replaced others; and yet again it would not be sensible to return all versions of those Features). An important requirement for version management is support of context: this is a client-specified property related to metadata access requests that is used to select the appropriate versions.

A related problem is the lack of a consistent mechanism for determining the status of versions of models or artifacts with respect to a development lifecycle (for example draft->approved->unit-tested->system-tested->live->withdrawn). This is often the most useful way of specifying a context (see previous paragraph) and to control the operations that may be applied to the metadata (e.g., to prohibit changes to the model for the 'live' version).

3.8.4 Qvt

See Section 4.3

3.8.5 mofm2t

This specification defines the MOF to Text Template Language (Mof2Text), version 1.0. Mof2Text is aligned with UML 2.0, MOF 2.0, and OCL 2.0.

Conformance

There are four levels of compliance as shown below. A compliance level is defined in terms of the supported syntax and features.

Syntax–Features	Core	Advanced
Abstract	Minimal	Intermediate
Concrete	Basic	Complete

- Abstract syntax compliance: The tool can read and interpret Mof2Text specifications in model form.
- Concrete syntax compliance: The tool can read and execute Mof2Text specifications in concrete syntax form. A tool supporting the concrete syntax also supports the abstract syntax.
- Core feature compliance: The tool supports core language features namely Template, Query, and Module.
- Advanced feature compliance: In addition to the core features, the tool also supports advanced features namely Module extension, Template Overriding, Text mode switching, and Macros.

3.8.6 OCL

See Chapter 2.

Chapter 4. Model Transformation

Software engineering is a dynamic and evolving discipline. It involves the continuous creation, maintenance, and improvement of software systems. Even after its release and finalization, software often requires updates and upgrades to adapt to new technologies, user needs, or environmental changes.

Transformation is a fundamental concept that predates model-driven engineering (MDE). It refers to the process of modifying or evolving software and components, whether structural, behavioral, or platform-related, to support ongoing development and maintenance. This concept is essential to software systems lifecycle management.

Model-Driven Engineering builds upon the traditional notion of transformation by introducing two critical concepts:

1. **Formalism**
   MDE provides a rigorous and structured framework for defining models and the rules for transforming them. This formalism ensures consistency, correctness, and traceability in the transformation process.
2. **Automation**
   MDE promotes the use of automated tools to perform model transformations. Automation reduces manual effort, minimizes human error, and accelerates the development process.

4.1 Definitions

A model transformation can be defined as a mapping between entities from one or more models (called input models) to one or more models (called output models).

The distinction between input and output models is purely convention-based, tied to the transformation's execution context in practice. Fundamentally, however, the transformation represents a relationship (or association) between two sets of models regardless of the transformation direction.

The execution of a transformation is transient—it merely facilitates the transition from input to output models (There is no permanent entity of a transformation). The metamodel of the transformation is the formal definition of these mappings and it is permanent.

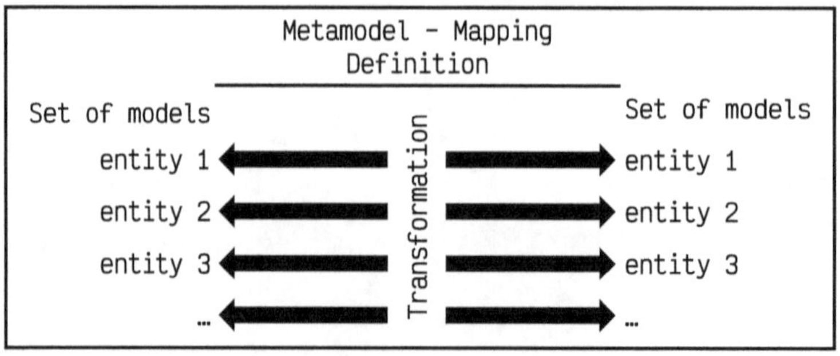

4.2 Classification of Transformations

To master the transformation of models, thus allowing a better understanding of requirements, a better design of solutions, and better maintenance and adaptation to changes, it is necessary to define the elements of the transformations and to classify them.

4.2.1 Model-Type Based classification

To choose the right theoretical tools to specify the transformation, and to choose the tools to implement a transformation, it is necessary to define the models involved in the transformation. Models can be classified into:

- textual models (defined as sequences of symbols allowing linear interpretation);
- Non-textual models (which cannot be defined as a serialization of information, and require a predefined interpretation in the metamodel).

The design and implementation tools available for these two types of models do not have the same complexity or level of difficulty, which separates transformations based on the type of model in terms of difficulty and complexity. Depending on the types of models involved in the transformation, we can have four types of transformation:

4.2.1.1 Text-to-Text Transformations

Text-to-Text transformations are used to convert one textual-based (sequence of symbols) representation into another. These transformations are generally applied in tasks such as translation (code or language), refactoring, reformatting, or transforming configuration files into different syntactic forms.

This type of transformation is the simplest and easiest to design and implement.

Definition

- A **Text-to-Text (T2T) Transformation** processes an input text-based models (**$T1_i$**) and produces transformed text-based models (**$T2_j$**). This can be for migration to new technology, optimization of code, or syntax adaptation. The transformation does not guarantee reciprocal return; it may preserve or modify the underlying semantics.

Common Use Cases

- **Source Code Refactoring and Rewriting** automatically reformats, optimizes, or restructures existing code without changing its behavior (renaming variables or restructuring control flow).
- **Language-to-Language Translation** converts code written in one programming language into another (e.g., from Java to C#, or from SQL to NoSQL query formats).
- **Syntactic Transformations for Migration** translates old configuration or script formats into new standards or platforms.
- **Documentation Format Conversion** transforms technical documentation between different formats (e.g., Markdown to LaTeX or HTML).

T2T Tools and Frameworks

- **XSLT** (Extensible Stylesheet Language Transformations) – Is a T2T tool designed for transforming XML documents into other formats including: XML, HTML, or plain text formats.

- **StringTemplate** – A Java template engine for generating structured text (e.g., source code, web pages).
- **Sed** (Stream Editor), **AWK** (named after its creators: Aho, Weinberger, Kernighan)**, or scripting languages (Python)** – Used for custom text processing and transformation scripts.
- **ANTLR** (ANother Tool for Language Recognition – with StringTemplate) – Used for parsing and generating text from structured languages.

4.2.1.2 Model-to-Model Transformations

Model-to-Model transformations are a core concept in Model-Driven Engineering (MDE), where one model is systematically converted into another, enabling automation, analysis, or refinement in the development process regardless the type of the model.

Definition

- A **Model-to-Model (M2M) Transformation** is a process that takes source models (**$M1_i$**), conforming to metamodels (**$MM1_i$**), and produces target models (**$M2_j$**).
- The target models (**$M2_j$**) may conform to the same input metamodels (**$MM1_i$**) or to different metamodels (**$MM2_j$**).

Common Examples

- **Refactoring a UML Class Diagram:** Such a transformation improves the structure of a class diagram without altering its semantics, often to enhance readability, maintainability, or design quality.
- **Converting a Platform-Independent Model (PIM) to a Platform-Specific Model (PSM)**: In this case, the transformation translates abstract system models into concrete implementations based on a specific platform (e.g., Java EE, .NET).
- **Translating BPMN Models into Petri Nets**: It enables formal analysis (e.g., deadlock detection, reachability) by mapping Business Process Model and Notation (BPMN) models to Petri nets.
- **Transforming State Machine Models into Sequence Diagrams:** In this example, we convert behavioral state transitions into interaction sequences between objects, aiding in understanding runtime behavior.

M2M Transformation Tools and Languages

- **ATL (Atlas Transformation Language)** – Supporting declarative and imperative hybrid language for model transformation.
- **QVT (Query/View/Transformation)** – An OMG transformation descriptor standard supporting model queries and transformations (includes QVT-Operational, QVT-Relations).
- **Henshin** – A rule-based transformation language for EMF models using graph transformation concepts.
- **VIATRA** – A model transformation framework integrating pattern matching and transformation for reactive or incremental systems.

4.2.1.3 Model-to-Text Transformations

Model-to-Text transformations are used to generate textual artifacts (sequential data) from abstract non-textual models. These transformations are essential in automating code generation, documentation, and configuration tasks within Model-Driven Development. This type of transformation is quite simple and straightforward to describe.

Definition

- A **Model-to-Text (M2T) Transformation** is a process that produces textual (**T_i**) outputs (Such as source code, documentation, configuration files) from models (**M_j**) conforming to metamodels (**MM_j**).

Common Use Cases

- **Code Generation from UML Models:** In this case, the transformation automatically generates source code from design models, such as generating Java classes from UML class diagrams.
- **Documentation Generation**: Production of structured textual documentation from system models, such as producing HTML documentation for model descriptions.
- **Configuration Files and Deployment Descriptors**: This transformation generates system-specific configurations required files for deployment, often from architectural or platform models. Such as a transformation that produces configuration files required for system deployment based on abstract models describing application structure and deployment needs.

M2T Transformation Tools and Languages

- **Acceleo** – An Eclipse-based tool implementing the MOFM2T standard, used for generating code from EMF models.
- **Xtend** – A flexible and expressive language for code generation that integrates well with Java.
- **EGL (Epsilon Generation Language)** – Part of the Epsilon platform, used for generating custom text from models.

4.2.1.4 Text-to-Model Transformations

Text-to-Model transformations enable the automatic creation of models from textual input. This is particularly useful in processing domain-specific languages, migrating legacy formats, and supporting reverse engineering in Model-Driven Engineering (MDE).

This type of transformation is the strongest and the most difficult to design and implement.

Definition

- A **Text-to-Model (T2M) Transformation** parses textual inputs (**T_i**) (a sequence of symbols) and produces corresponding models (**M_j**) that conforms to specific metamodels (**MM_j**).

Common Use Cases

- **Parsing Domain-Specific Languages (DSLs)** to convert domain-specific textual notations into models that can be analyzed or transformed further.

- **Reverse Engineering Source Code** to extract abstract models (e.g., UML) from existing source code for analysis or modernization.
- **Importing Legacy Configuration Files** that transform outdated or proprietary configuration files into structured models for migration to new platforms or standards. An example can be parsing a custom DSL into an EMF (Eclipse Modeling Framework) model for integration into a model transformation workflow.

T2M Transformation Tools and Frameworks

- **Xtext** – Framework for developing DSLs that automatically provides a parser and an EMF-based model representation.
- **EMFText** – Allows the definition of textual syntaxes for EMF models and generates parsers for them.
- **ANTLR + Custom Parsers** – A powerful parser generator used to build custom text parsers that can be linked to metamodels manually.

4.2.2 Endogenous and Exogenous Transformations

A transformation is said to be **endogenous** when its source and target models conform to the same metamodels. For example, code refactoring or optimization are considered endogenous transformations. The transformation is then said to operate in the same technological space.

Conversely, a transformation is said to be **exogenous** when its source and target models conform to different metamodels. This is generally the case for translation-type transformations, platform mapping, and reverse engineering. Such transformations are then said to operate in different technological spaces.

Endogenous transformations involve rewriting or reformulating models according to the same rules: within the same metamodel. These transformations generally require less structural effort while requiring sophisticated logic to ensure the validity, relevance, and semantic preservation of the changes.

In the other hand, exogenous transformations operate between different metamodels by a complete reformulation according to new distinct rules. Although they often require more implementation effort, their rationale and foundation are generally more explicit thanks to the distinct source and target representations.

4.2.3 6.2 Horizontal and Vertical Transformations

A transformation is said to be **horizontal** when the source and target models are at the same level of abstraction. Examples include the transformation of a class diagram into a component diagram, or the migration of a program from Java to C++: In the first case, both models are solution design models, and in the second, the program is rewritten in another language while maintaining the same level, which is the solution formulation.

Conversely, a transformation is said to be **vertical** when it involves models at different levels of abstraction. A typical example is the refinement of a PIM model into another PSM, where a high-level abstract model is systematically transformed into a more detailed and concrete representation linked to a technical platform.

4.2.4 Syntactic and Semantic Transformations

A transformation is considered **syntactic**[3] when it relies uniquely on the structural or grammatical aspects of the model, without interpreting its meaning or semantics. Such transformations focus on format and the representation of the model entities rather than their behavior or intent. An example of such a transformation is generating an abstract syntax tree (AST) from source code using a parser; or converting a UML class diagram from XML-based format (XMI-based file) preserving structure without analyzing model semantics.

In contrast, a transformation is considered as semantic when it takes into account the meaning and intended behavior of the model elements. These transformations go beyond surface structure and aim to preserve or modify the model's semantics. For example, transforming a UML state machine into executable code, or checking behavioral consistency between a UML sequence diagram and a state machine, involves semantic transformation, as it requires understanding the dynamic behavior represented in the models.

4.2.5 Bidirectional and Unidirectional Transformations

A transformation is called **bidirectional** when every model involved can serve as both a source and a target, enabling modifications to propagate in the two directions. Here are two examples of bidirectional transformation:

- *Database to view synchronization*: The changes made to either the database schema or its view (Such a simplified User–Interface representation UI) can update the other.
- *Model-code co-evolution*: Adjustments in a UML diagram automatically update the source code, and vice versa.

While such transformations maintain consistency, they aren't always lossless (converting XML to SON and vice versa may discard comments or formatting).

Conversely, a **unidirectional** transformation propagates changes in one direction only, making reverse synchronization impossible. Here are two examples of unidirectional transformation:

- Program Compilation: The transformation of source code (C program) to machine code is irreversible.
- PDF generation: Moving from a LaTeX file to a PDF one does not allow to reconstruct the original LaTeX perfectly.

Bidirectional transformations are essential in tools and solutions requiring dynamic synchronization (maintaining two models in the same work level), like collaborative software design platforms.

---

[3] Common synonym or closely related terms for **syntactic transformation** are:
Structure-preserving transformation; Format-based transformation; Surface-level transformation; Grammar-driven transformation; Representation-level transformation

4.3 Example of transformation descriptor: QVT

4.3.1 The QVT Standard (OMG)

This section presents the official QVT standard as defined by the Object Management Group (OMG). It establishes the conceptual foundations for model transformation in Model-Driven Architecture (MDA) and serves as a connection between abstract models and their concrete realizations.

4.3.1.1 Overview of QVT (Query/View/Transformation)

To understand what QVT is, its role in IDM, and how it supports transformation tasks at different levels of abstraction, it is necessary to define certain related concepts, outline the framework for its use, and position QVT within the development cycle.

Key concepts:

QVT defines a set of languages for describing model transformations that conform to MOF-based metamodels (see Chapter 3).

As part of the OMG MDA initiative, QVT enables the implementation of model transformations in toolchains involving platform-independent (PIM) and platform-specific (PSM) models.

QVT stands for Query, View, and Transformation. These three concepts define the transformation description mechanism adopted by this approach, namely:

Queries: Used to extract or filter information from the models that are the subject of the defined transformation. Views: Defined to present models differently or partially, without modifying them for the purpose of the transformation in question.

The transformation itself defines correspondences between the source and target models (unidirectional or bidirectional).

Use cases:

QVT is used in any transformation designed by mapping between models. A classic use case is the mapping between UML class models and relational database schemas. A second example is the mapping between state machines in Petri nets.

QVT's position in the model lifecycle:

QVT can be used to describe transformations at almost any level of abstraction: for example, between analysis, design, and implementation models, or between high-level business models and technical artifacts. However, describing transformations between base-level models, such as transformations defining source code compilation or code optimization, is not as straightforward in QVT.

4.3.1.2 The three QVT languages: QVT-Core, QVT-Relations, QVT-Operational

I will present and attempt to differentiate the three sublanguages defined by the QVT standard:

1. QVT-Core

This is the fundamental, low-level language, designed as a target for other QVT languages. It is a declarative and structural language, but primarily theoretical and rarely used directly. It acts as an intermediate representation in QVT-R and QVT-O implementations.

2. QVT-Relations (QVT-R)

This is a high-level, declarative language for specifying model transformations via relations between them. It is the most widely used in practice.

It uses domains to describe the source and target models and relations that specify the correspondence between elements of the input and output models. When and Where clauses provide conditions and constraints on these correspondences to better formalize the application of the transformation. QVT-R supports bidirectionality by default (by definition).

This language is ideal for synchronizing similar models following the same definition paradigm. This synchronization is defined by a declarative correspondence between two metamodels.

3. QVT-Operational (QVT-O)

This is the imperative version, enabling step-by-step model transformation operations. It uses imperative constructs such as loops, conditions, and variables to specify structures in mapping operations.

It can also invoke wizards and procedures and allows in-place transformation and precise execution control.

This language is suitable for complex transformations involving logic, conditions, or sequencing.

4.3.2 Comparatives tables

Feature	**QVT-Relations**	**QVT-Operational**
Paradigm	Declarative	Imperative
Bidirectional	Yes – by definition	No (manually handled)
Level of abstraction	High	Medium to Low
Tooling support	Limited / graphical	Strong (**QVTo** engine)
Use cases	Simple mapping/sync	Complex logic, code generation

Table 4 Comparative summary between QVT languages

Language	**Type**	**Style**	**Tooling**	**Key Characteristics**
QVT-R	Declarative	Graph-based	Eclipse/Medini	Bidirectional – OMG standard
QVT-O	Imperative	Script-like	Eclipse QVTo	Imperative control flow
ATL	Hybrid	Rule-based	Eclipse ATL	Widely adopted – declarative core, imperative helpers
ETL	Hybrid	Rule-based	Epsilon Platform	Built-in model management; reusable operations
Xtend	General-purpose	Textual templates	Eclipse Xtend	Templating for model-to-text (M2T); flexible syntax

Table 5 Comparative summary between Transformation Languages

4.3.3 QVT-Core

QVT-Core is the foundational layer of the OMG-defined QVT transformation languages. It provides a minimal formal foundation upon which the QVT-Relations (QVT-R) and QVT-

Operational (QVT-O) languages are built. Although not commonly used directly in practice, a good understanding of QVT-Core is essential for grasping the formal semantics and traceability mechanisms of higher-level QVT languages.

4.3.3.1 QVT-Core syntax and semantics

To understand the abstract syntax and formal semantics of QVT-Core, a minimal transformation language, one must understand its key concepts, abstract syntax, and semantics.

Key concepts:

QVT-Core transformations are defined as sets of relations between the source and target models, where each relation involves a pattern match on the models and specifies the correspondence of the corresponding elements. The adopted language is purely declarative and defined according to graph transformation semantics.

Abstract syntax (A simplified view):

The transformation is defined by a set of relational rules.

The relation is defined as correspondences between domain patterns.

A domain is any pattern of structured objects (often trees or graphs) that conforms to a metamodel.

A pattern is a structural model, possibly accompanied by constraints (such as OCL constraints).

Semantics Overview:

A transformation is executed by pattern matching on the source model and instantiating the target elements as specified in the relation. Trace objects are implicitly generated to maintain consistency and enable bidirectional evaluation.

"Verify" and "Apply" modes are used to determine whether the transformation is validated or executed.

In the following example, this relation associates a *SourceClass* object with name *mn* and creates a *TargetClass* object with the same label:

```
relation R {
  domain source s : SourceClass { name = mn };
  domain target t : TargetClass { label = mn };
}
```

4.3.3.2 Transformation rules, patterns, and traceability

Here, I present the transformation logic and how it is expressed through rules, as well as how traceability is inherently supported in QVT-Core.

Transformation Rules:

Rules constitute the central unit of a transformation and are composed of:

- Domain models for the source and target models;
- Guards or constraints (e.g., OCL expressions);
- Optional default values, bindings, and object creation logic.

Each rule defines a mapping between the source and target elements.

Patterns:
Patterns describe the model structure using tree-like object graphs. These patterns can be mapped (in the source) or created and applied (in the target). Bindings are used to reference object attributes or navigation paths.
Traceability:
A trace object is created for each relation applied during a transformation. The trace object record contains:
- The source and target instances involved.
- The transformation rules applied.
- The parameters used in applying the transformation.

This traceability allows the transformation to support:
- Bidirectional transformations.
- Incremental updates.
- And possibly reverse engineering.

4.3.3.3 Limitations and typical use cases

Abstraction is the major limitation of QVT-Core, which makes it unsuitable for direct use by practitioners due to its lack of syntactic complexity and readability.
For **low-level transformations**, it requires very fine-grained specification of transformations. The lack of built-in control structures means it does not support imperative logic such as conditionals, loops, or user-defined functions.
All these limitations **impact related tools**; most tools (such as Eclipse QVTo) do not support direct editing or debugging of QVT-Core.
Use cases:
Despite its abstraction, QVT-Core is essential for:

- **Formal semantics:** It is used as a formal basis for defining the semantics of QVT-R and QVT-O.
- **Model Transformation Engines:** Transformation tools can compile QVT-R into QVT-Core as an intermediate representation.
- **Research and Analysis:** It is used in academic contexts to study transformation correctness, bidirectionality, or trace semantics.

4.3.4 QVT-Relations (QVT-R)

QVT-Relations (QVT-R) is the declarative component of the QVT standard for model transformation, defined and standardized by the Object Management Group (OMG). It allows transformations between models to be expressed declaratively and bidirectionally, specifying what should be transformed rather than how; it is therefore a transformation descriptor and not a solution design tool. It is particularly useful when transformations need to be synchronized or when changes in one model need to be reflected in another.

4.3.4.1 Declarative transformations and relational semantics

Declarative transformations focus on describing the relations between the source and target models rather than prescribing a sequence of transformation steps. In QVT-R:

- ✓ Relations define a condition that must be met between elements of the source and target models.
- ✓ Relational semantics means that transformations rely on logical constraints rather than procedural operations.

The key features of any QVT-R transformation description are:

- ✓ High-level abstraction: Users specify the correspondence that must exist between elements of different models.
- ✓ Bidirectionality: The same description can be used to transform from source to target or vice versa, as the relation is defined regardless of the direction in which the transformation is applied.
- ✓ Consistency preservation: Ensures model consistency according to the defined relation.

Consider the classic example of mapping between a class diagram and a relational database. In this case, if a UML class is to be translated into a table in a relational model, QVT-R expresses the correspondence as a relation, not a sequence of steps.

4.3.4.2 Syntax: domains, relations, when/where clauses

The syntax of this language is based on the following concepts: Domains, relations and when/where clauses.

Domains

Each relation has one or more domains, which represent elements of the source and target models involved in the transformation. A domain describes:

- The model to which it belongs (source or target);
- A pattern to which the elements of this model must match.

Relations

A relation is a central unit of QVT-R. It connects the elements of one or more domains and defines their relations.

```
relation ClassToTable {
  domain source c : uml::Class;
  domain target t : rdbms::Table {
    name = c.name;
  }
}
```

When Clause

Specifies a precondition for applying the relation. It typically refers to other relations or model conditions that must be met before calling the current relation.

```
when {
  c.isPersistent = true;
}
```

Where Clause

Used for postconditions or subrelations to establish additional matches.

```
where {
  ClassAttributesToColumns(c.attributes, t.columns);
}
```

4.3.4.3 Graphical vs textual representations

QVT-R supports both graphical and textual syntaxes.

Graphical syntax

This is generally used in Eclipse-based tools, such as Eclipse QVTo or Medini QVT, where relationships and domains are visualized as diagrams to make the description more intuitive for non-programmers. This graphical visualization allows for an understanding of the overall structure.

The classic example of a graphical representation of transformation is the mapping between a class diagram and a relational database (See Figure 13):

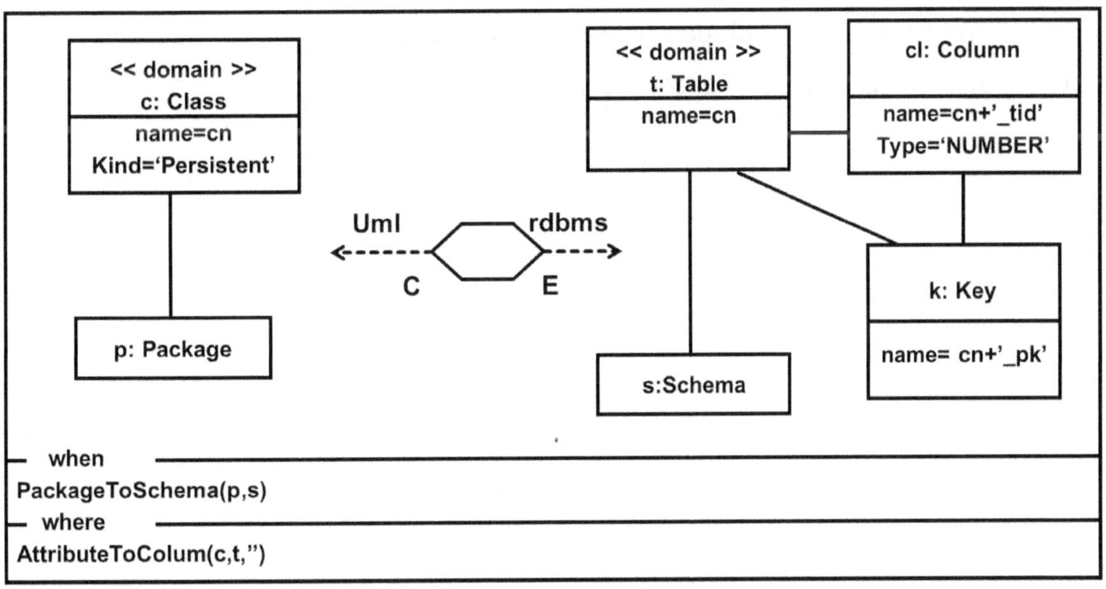

Figure 13 Graphical Notation of QVT-R Transformation Example

Textual syntax

This is a DSL (Domain-Specific Language) that allows for better management of large-scale transformations. This language is optimized for version control and automation and also allows advanced constructs such as when/where clauses, recursive calls, etc.

4.3.4.4 Bidirectional transformations and traceability

QVT-R is inherently **bidirectional**; a relation can be evaluated in forward (from source to target) or reverse (from target to source) mode without disrupting definitions and concepts. This is useful in consistency-maintaining scenarios such as model synchronization, round-trip engineering, and coevolution.

For **traceability**, each transformation execution generates a model trace. This trace records the applied relations and element mapping, allowing for incremental transformations and rollbacks.

4.3.4.5 Case Study: FSM to Petri Net Transformation

Transforming a finite state machine into a Petri net can serve as an example of applying QVT-R to describe transformations. Let's start by defining the two models:

A simplified **finite state machine** is composed of: **States**, **Transitions**, **Initial State** and **Final States.**

A simplified **Petri net**, on the other hand, is composed of: **Places**, **Transitions** (with a different meaning than finite state machines) and **Arcs** (partially equivalent to finite state machine transitions)

The objective of this example is to transform a finite state machine model into a corresponding Petri net model by applying these pattern matches:

- Transforming **States** into **Places**
- Finite State Machine **Transitions** into Petri **Transitions**
- Arcs connect entry/exit places to Petri **transitions**

The textual solution could be as follow

```
relation StateToPlace {
  domain source s : fsm::State;
  domain target p : petri::Place {
    name = s.name;
  }
}
relation TransitionToPetriTransition {
  domain source t : fsm::Transition {
    source = s1 : fsm::State,
    target = s2 : fsm::State
  };
  domain target pt : petri::Transition {
    name = t.name;
  }
  where {
    ArcFromStateToTransition(s1, pt);
    ArcFromTransitionToState(pt, s2);
  }
}
relation ArcFromStateToTransition {
  domain source s : fsm::State;
  domain target a : petri::Arc {
    source = p : petri::Place,
    target = pt : petri::Transition
  }
  when {
    StateToPlace(s, p);
  }
}
relation ArcFromTransitionToState {
  domain source s : fsm::State;
  domain target a : petri::Arc {
    source = pt : petri::Transition,
    target = p : petri::Place
  }
  when {
    StateToPlace(s, p);
  }
}
```

4.3.5 QVT-Operational (QVT-O)

QVT-Operational (QVT-O) is an imperative transformation language defined by the OMG as part of the QVT standard. While QVT-Relations (QVT-R) is declarative and focuses on specifying the elements to be transformed, QVT-O focuses on how transformations are executed, providing precise step-by-step control over the transformation process.

QVT-O is particularly suited for scenarios requiring complex control flow, advanced computations, or procedural logic that is difficult to express in a purely declarative style where patterns are difficult to discern.

4.3.5.1 Imperative model transformations

Imperative model transformations explicitly define the steps to follow in relation to a linear reading of the input model. Unlike declarative approaches, which rely on constraints and relationships, imperative approaches describe precise procedures for manipulating the model.

Key features of the language:

- ✓ This language provides the tools for imperative programming through explicit control flows (such as loops and conditions).
- ✓ Side effects are allowed and often necessary, such as for object creation or property modifications.
- ✓ This language is suitable for transformations with complex logic, the creation of conditional objects, or the sequencing of dependent transformations.

Examples requiring such an imperative approach include transformations requiring conditional rules or detailed temporary trace data, such as in the case of in-place model migrations where procedural processing is performed under parameter and variable conditions.

4.3.5.2 Syntax and structure of QVT-O

This language is written in an OCL-based imperative syntax and arranged around **transformation modules** containing **mapping operations** and optionally **helpers** or **libraries**. The key structural elements of this language are:

- **Transformation**: The main unit where mappings are defined.
- **Mapping**: The core transformation rule that defines how a source model is transformed into a target model.
- **Helper**: A reusable function or attribute used to simplify logic.
- **Intermediate Classes**: Temporary trace elements that allow tracking of the transformation process.

```
transformation SampleTrans(source: SourceMM, target: TargetMM);
mapping SourceElement::toTargetElement() : TargetElement {
    init {
        self.targetElement.name := self.name;
    }
    population {
        // Additional logic or nested mappings
    }
}
// Control structures supported:
// if, else, while, for, return
// checkonly vs enforce modes
// init and population sections within mappings
```

4.3.5.3 Libraries, helpers, mapping operations

QVT-O indorses modularity and code reuse through the use of libraries and helpers. In **libraries**, we define reusable operations, types, or constants and can be imported into transformation modules.

```
library MathLib {
    helper def add(x: Integer, y: Integer): Integer = x + y;
}
```

Helpers are used to encapsulate computation logic, and can be defined globally or within mappings. There are two types of Helpers: Attribute helpers (That return values) and Operation helpers (That execute logic with parameters):

```
helper def computeName(source: SourceElement): String {
    return source.firstName + ' ' + source.lastName;
}
```

Mapping Operations are used to define transformation rules for specific types and can include inheritance (overriding or extending mappings) or invoked explicitly or matched by type automatically.

```
mapping SourceType::transform() : TargetType {
    init {
        result.name := self.computeName();
    }
}
```

4.3.5.4 Integration with QVT-R

QVT-O and QVT-R can be **integrated** together to enable transformations leveraging both declarative and imperative paradigms (Hybrid). This can help:

- Using QVT-R to declare high-level relationships (Declarative Mode).
- Using QVT-O for fine-grained control when declarative constraints are insufficient (Imperative Mode).
- Shared metamodels and traceability links enable interoperability between systems.

As for integration mechanisms, QVT-O can invoke relationships defined in QVT-R and vice versa without any restrictions. The resulting transformations are then in mixed mode (e.g., QVT-R for mapping structural-organizational parts, and QVT-O for logic or computed attributes).

An **example** of a classic integration scenario is using QVT-R to define structure defined by mapping classes and associations. And the delegation of the calculation of complex attributes or conditional logic to QVT-O.

4.3.5.5 Error handling and execution control

Like any imperative paradigm, QVT-O provides mechanisms for error handling and controlling the execution flow of transformations.

For error handling, try-catch blocks can be used to handle exceptions to recognize and correct crashes. Validation conditions can also be used in mappings and helpers (assertions). Transformation errors can also be reported using logs or error-generating constructs.

```
try {
    // risky operation
} catch (e: Exception) {
    log("Error occurred: " + e.message);
}
```

Transformation **execution is controlled** by standard imperative structures such as *return, continue, break, if, while*.

The execution order can be explicitly managed by: Mapping invocations, Conditional rule execution and Mapping dependencies.

Trace templates are automatically generated and can be used for transformation debugging. Tools like Eclipse QVTo allow visual debugging and on-demand stepping.

Finally, as with any imperative language, it is always best to use logging and traceability for error diagnosis. It is also best to modularize complex mappings as much as possible and to strategically combine QVT-R and QVT-O for greater clarity and efficiency.

4.4 Practical Tools for Model Transformation

For hands-on work in model transformation (including all the concepts and paradigms), here are essential tools categorized by their primary use case:

Grammar-Based & Parser-Driven Tools

- *ANTLR (ANother Tool for Language Recognition):* Generates parsers/lexers for DSLs and programming languages.

  Supports bidirectional transformations via grammar rules with **StringTemplate** (templating engine).

  - *Xtext (Eclipse):* Integrates with ANTLR to create full IDE support for DSLs, including code generation.

XML/Structured Data Transformations

- *XSLT (Extensible Stylesheet Language Transformations):* Standard for XML-to-XML or XML-to-text (model-to-code for example).

  The XSLT 3.0 supports higher-order functions and streaming for complex transformations.

- *QVT (Query/View/Transformation):* OMG (Object Management Group) standard for model-to-model transformations (UML to relational database for example).

Low-Level Text/Data Processing

- *Sed (Stream Editor) & AWK:* Lightweight scripting for preprocessing/unidirectional text transformations (For example: Normalizing logs or config files before model ingestion).

General-Purpose Scripting

- *Python (with libraries like PyEcore, TextX, lxml):* Rapid prototyping of custom transformations (e.g., CSV→JSON, DSL→API specs).
- *JavaScript/TypeScript (with chevrotain, nearley):* Web-based tooling for in-browser model transformations.

Specialized Model Transformation Frameworks

- *Eclipse Modeling Framework (EMF) + ATL (Atlas Transformation Language):* Industry-standard for M2M (Model-to-Model) in Eclipse ecosystems.
- *Henshin (Eclipse):* Graph-based transformations for EMF models.
- TXL: Source-to-source transformation for legacy code modernization.

Bidirectional Focus

- *BXtend (extension of Xtend for bx):* Research tool for bidirectional model synchronization.
- *QVT-R (QVT Relations):* Declarative bidirectional mappings (part of the QVT standard).

Chapter 5. Models and Execution

In model-driven engineering (**MDE**), models are the fundamental and primary artifacts that capture the structure, behavior, and constraints of systems at various levels of abstraction, from reflection to implementation and deployment. However, to be truly useful and usable, models must not only represent systems but also be executable, verifiable, and formally defined. This chapter, **Models and Execution**, explores the crucial transition from models—by definition static—to dynamic, analyzable, and semantically accurate representations. We begin by examining **model execution and simulation**, where abstract models are redefined as executable systems. Next, we delve into **model verification, validation, and control**, ensuring correctness and consistency before use. The chapter then addresses **full model specification**, emphasizing the need for unambiguous and constraint-rich models. Finally, we explore **formal semantics**—axiomatic, operational, and denotational—that provide rigorous mathematical foundations for model interpretation. This chapter equips students with the skills needed to bridge the gap between conceptual modeling and real-world execution in MDE.

5.1 Execution/Simulation

Simulation and execution are fundamental techniques in Computer Science and particularly in Model-Driven Engineering (MDE) that enable engineers to analyze, test, and validate system models before actual implementation and deployment. This section explores how models are executed or simulated to predict the behavior of the target product, reduce development risks, and improve design quality.

5.1.1 Purpose of Simulation and Execution

Model execution serves several key purposes in MDE:

- **Early Validation**: Ensures the correctness and the validity of the models early in the development cycle.
- **Behavioral Prediction**: Provides insight into how the system would behave under certain inputs or conditions.
- **Debugging**: Helps identify design flaws, failures or inconsistencies before generating code.
- **Requirements Checking**: Confirms that the designed models meet the functional and non-functional initial requirements.
- **Performance Estimation**: Predicts different resource usage, timing, or responsiveness.

5.1.2 Types of Models and Execution Semantics

Execution semantics vary across different models. By execution, we mean to evaluate the behavior of some computational entity over logical time—that is, iterations or state changes in the machine, as opposed to physical time measured in minutes or seconds. For a compiled program, execution is straightforward and trivial. But for a conceptual model, specifying its behavior over time, and therefore its semantics, is not necessarily easy. This is why we distinguish three kinds of models, based on how they are defined when dealing with dynamic or evolutionary aspects:

- **Structural models (such as class diagrams):** Are generally not directly executable because they lack a dynamic component in their definitions. However, to understand their behavior over time, it is necessary to define their contexts of use. Class diagrams, for example, are instantiated for use; therefore, their execution is linked to the behavior of their instances, which are objects, through changes in attribute values and calls to different methods. Understanding the behavior of static models, then, involves tracking the behavior of the instances.
- **Behavioral models (such as state machines, activity diagrams, or Petri nets):** Are by definition suited to both execution and simulation because their specification includes a dynamic component through transitions and state changes, thus defining an evolution over time that is analogous to program execution.
- **Hybrid models:** Combine structural and behavioral aspects, such as SysML or AADL. In this case, the evolution over time and the change of state of static instances define the evolution and behavior of the overall model.

5.1.3 Simulation Techniques

Simulation techniques enable the execution and analysis of models at various levels of abstraction, ranging from analysis and design to implementation and deployment. Here are some common approaches:

5.1.3.1 Interpretation:

A dedicated model interpreter directly executes the model by dynamically applying its semantic rules. This approach is often used for state machines, Petri nets, and other formal models, where an interpreter evaluates transitions and state changes in real time to validate and correct the model based on the interpretation.

5.1.3.2 Code Generation and Execution:

In this approach, the model is automatically transformed into executable source code (e.g., C++, Java, Python) and then compiled or interpreted. This method improves performance and enables integration with existing software systems. Tools such as MATLAB/Simulink and Xtext often use this technique. This technique is more suited to solution and implementation models than to preliminary models in projects.

5.1.3.3 Co-simulation:

Multiple simulators (e.g., Simulink + Functional Mock-Up Interface (FMI)) work together to simulate heterogeneous systems. Each component can use a different modeling formalism (e.g., continuous-time or discrete events), and synchronization mechanisms ensure consistent interaction.

5.1.3.4 Trace-based simulation:

Instead of a full execution, this method generates and analyzes execution traces, i.e., sequences of states or events representing possible behaviors. It is useful for verification, debugging, and exploring system dynamics without real-time constraints.

Each technique presents tradeoffs in terms of flexibility, performance, and fidelity, depending on the modeling context.

5.1.4 Tools and Frameworks

Here are some common MDE tools that support model simulation and execution:

- **Eclipse Modeling Framework (EMF)** with **Xtext**, **QVTo**, or **Xtend**
- **fUML (Foundational UML)** and **PSCS (Precise Semantics of UML Composite Structures)** for precise behavioral simulation
- **Papyrus** with **Moka** (model execution engine for fUML)
- **AToM**, **Yakindu**, **Simulink**, and **UPPAAL** for specific domains like control systems and timed automata
- **Acceleo** for model-to-code generation

5.1.5 Practical example: Executing a State Machine Model

Consider the following UML state machine modeling a door system:

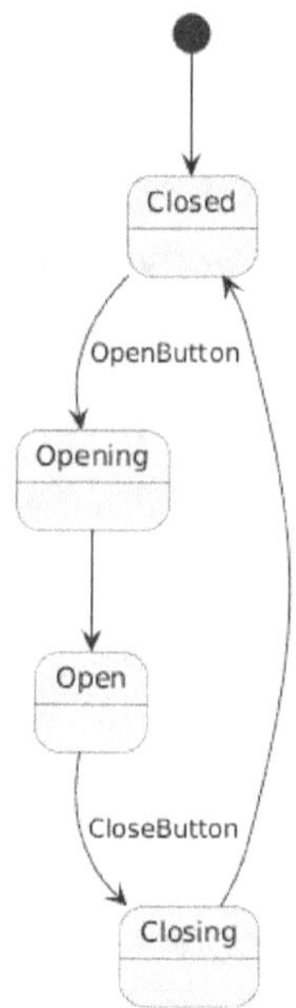


```
States: Closed, Opening, Open, Closing
Events: OpenButton, CloseButton
Transitions:
- Closed --(OpenButton)--> Opening
- Opening --> Open
- Open --(CloseButton)--> Closing
- Closing --> Closed
```

The steps for executing this model are as follows:

1. The interpreter reads the initial state (`Closed`).
2. On `OpenButton` event, transition fires: move to `Opening`.
3. After a delay or completion condition, state changes to `Open`.
4. On `CloseButton` event, transition to `Closing`.
5. Eventually back to `Closed`.

Simulation allows to verify event sequences, transition logic as well as time constraints if they exist.

5.1.6 Challenges and Considerations

Model simulation is a crucial step in any development process to analyze system behavior, but it presents several challenges to ensure accuracy, efficiency, and reliability.

5.1.6.1 Precision vs. Complexity

When discussing simulation or model execution, it is important to understand that the higher the fidelity of the models, capturing the finest details of system behavior, the more computational resources they require. Consequently, increased model complexity can slow down simulations, making iterative testing and validation more difficult or even impossible for the entire model.

Therefore, trade-offs must be found between accuracy and simulation speed, especially in real-time applications.

Mitigation strategies

- Use abstraction and simplification techniques where possible.
- Use multi-level modeling (e.g., hybrid models combining discrete-event and continuous-time simulations).

Some practical examples

- Computational Fluid Dynamics (CFD): High-resolution CFD models (e.g., ANSYS Fluent, OpenFOAM) simulate airflow over an aircraft wing with high accuracy, but require intensive computational resources.
- Electronic circuit simulation: SPICE tools (e.g., LTspice, Cadence PSpice) can become slow for large integrated circuits.

5.1.6.2 Scalability

Simulating large-scale system models (e.g., distributed networks, IoT ecosystems, or industrial processes) can be computationally expensive, calling into question the usefulness and throughput of such modeling. This challenge involves memory and processing limitations that can limit the size or resolution of the proposed models. In addition, parallel and distributed simulation techniques may be necessary, but they also pose synchronization challenges.

Mitigation strategies

- Exploit cloud computing or high-performance computing (HPC) clusters.
- Use modular and hierarchical modeling to decompose large systems into manageable sub-models.

Practical examples

- Network simulation: NS-3 and OMNeT++ simulate large communication networks but face extreme scalability challenges.
- Supply chain simulation: AnyLogic can model global logistics but may require cloud computing for optimization.

5.1.6.3 Non-determinism

Models such as Petri nets, concurrent state machines, or probabilistic systems can exhibit multiple valid behaviors due to non-deterministic transitions or race conditions. This raises reproducibility issues that complicate debugging and validation. The statistical methods (such as Monte Carlo simulations) may be necessary to explore possible outcomes.

Mitigation strategies

- Formal verification techniques (e.g., model checking) can help analyze all possible execution paths.
- Define clear constraints or priorities for transition rules to reduce ambiguity.

Practical examples

- Concurrent software verification: The Spin model checker analyzes multithreaded code to detect race conditions.
- Stochastic Petri nets: Tools such as CPN Tools simulate non-deterministic workflows.

5.1.6.4 Semantics Alignment:

Simulation procedure must ensure that the simulation semantics (the model's behavior with respect to its system representability) match the implementation semantics (the behavior of the real system). This correspondence is essential, but its implementation is often complex. This observation implies discrepancies that can lead to erroneous predictions or flawed system designs. Differences in timing, concurrency management, or event ordering can also introduce subtle bugs.

Mitigation strategies

- Perform rigorous model validation against real-world observations or reference implementations.
- Use standardized formalisms (e.g., UML, SysML) to maintain consistency between design and simulation.

Mitigation Strategies

- Co-simulation: Use of the Functional Mock-Up Interface (FMI) to combine different simulation tools.
- Model Calibration: Parameter tuning using real-world data (e.g., MATLAB's Simulink Design Optimization).
- Digital Twins: Continuous synchronization of simulations with real-world system data (e.g., Siemens Xcelerator).

Practical Examples

- Autonomous Vehicle Simulation: CARLA and Gazebo must accurately reflect real-world sensor noise and physics.
- Hardware-in-the-Loop (HIL): dSPACE and NI VeriStand validate embedded systems against simulated environments.

5.1.7 Benefits in the MDE Lifecycle

Overall, simulation bridges the gap between abstract models and concrete implementations, enhancing verification, validation, and refinement across all MDE phases. Simulation and execution complement other Model-Driven Engineering (MDE) activities in several key ways:

In Modeling, simulation provides immediate feedback and insight into design decisions, allowing actors to test and refine models early in the development process before deployment. By simulating system behavior and semantics, potential flaws or inefficiencies can be identified and adjusted before implementation, improving overall model quality.

In Analysis, simulation enables dynamic and real time property checking, such as verifying reachability, deadlock freedom, or other behavioral and dynamic constraints. Unlike static analysis alone, execution-based validation guarantees that the model behaves as expected (regarding the represented systm) under various runtime conditions, increasing confidence in the system's correctness.

In Transformation, and before applying model-to-model or model-to-text transformations, simulation helps validate the correctness of the source model. By executing the model, developers can confirm that its behavior aligns with current requirements, reducing the risk of propagating potential errors through subsequent transformations.

In Code Generation, the simulated behavior of a model serves as a reference for validating executable code generated. By comparing the execution traces of the model and the implemented system, developers can ensure that the code generated accurately reflects the intended design, improving consistency and reliability.

5.2 Verification, Validation, Model-Checking, Prototyping

In Model Driven Engineering (MDE), it is crucial to ensure the accuracy and reliability of models before their deployment. This section explores the main approaches used to evaluate models which are: verification, validation, model testing and prototyping.

5.2.1 Verification

In MDE, **verification** checks whether a given model is **correctly built** regarding its specifications and design rules. It answers the question: *"Are we building the model right ?"*

How to do it?

- **Formal Proofs:** Using mathematical logic to verify system properties on the model.
- **Static Analysis:** Examining the model's structure without execution (e.g., syntax checks).
- **Code Reviews & Inspections:** Manual or automated checks for consistency with requirements.

Example of verification approach

Verifying that a business process model follows BPMN (Business Process Model and Notation) rules.

5.2.2 Validation

Validation ensures that the model meets the user needs and the real-world requirements. It answers: *"Are we building the right model?"*

How to do it?

- **By simulation,** running the model under different test scenarios to compare with the expected behaviors.
- **By user Feedback,** involving stakeholders to evaluate model relevance.
- **By comparison with Real Data, t**esting against historical or experimental data.

Example of validation approach

Validating a predictive maintenance model by checking if its outputs match actual equipment failure records.

5.2.3 Model-Checking

Model-checking is an automated verification technique that exhaustively checks whether a model satisfies formal specifications (e.g., temporal logic properties).

How to do it?

- The model is represented as a **state-transition system**.
- Specifications are expressed in logic (e.g., LTL – Linear Temporal Logic).
- A model-checker explores all possible states to verify correctness.

Model-Checking guarantees correctness for all possible executions, and allow to provide counterexamples if properties are violated. However, it suffers from **state explosion** for large and complicated models.

Example of Model-Checking

Verifying that a concurrent system never enters a deadlock state.

5.2.4 Prototyping

Prototyping involves building a preliminary version of the system to evaluate feasibility, usability, and functionality before full development. We have two types of prototyping:

- **Throwaway Prototyping:** It is a quick model for concept validation, then it is discarded.
- **Evolutionary Prototyping:** It consists of a durable prototype iteratively refined into the final product.

This approach allows to early detection of design flaws, and enhances user involvement and feedback.

Example of prototyping

Developing a mock-up interface for a new e-commerce platform to test user interactions.

5.3 Complete Model Specification

Complete model specification helps tremendously in the context of model verification and execution. Incomplete models hamper automated reasoning, simulation, and validation. Completeness ensures that models are analyzable, verifiable, and executable under real-world conditions. To achieve a complete model specification, the following elements must be present:

- **Abstract syntax:** This is defined by a properly designed metamodel.
- **Concrete syntax:** This incorporates visual or textual representation (e.g., class diagrams, state diagrams).
- **Well-formedness rules:** This is captured using OCL or equivalent constraint languages.
- **Behavioral specification,** This consists of two aspects:
    1. State-based behavior (e.g., UML state machines).

2. Action-based behavior (e.g., activity diagrams, Petri nets).

- **Semantics:** The formal meaning that allows for analysis or execution.

Case Study - Simple Traffic Light System:

Abstract Syntax:

- States: {Red, Green, Yellow}
- Transitions: {Red → Green, Green → Yellow, Yellow → Red}

Well-Formedness:

- The model must contain exactly one initial state.
- There are no unreachable states.

Behavioral Model:

- State machine defining transitions with timing constraints.

Executable Semantics:

- Timed transitions implemented in xUML or fUML.
- Simulated using a model execution engine.

5.3.1.1 Modeling Challenges and Best Practices

- Overspecification and ambiguity must be avoided in the design process.
- Always try to modularize specifications to separate concerns and potential deviations.
- Use traceability links between syntax, constraints, and behavior.
- Ensure consistency between different views of the model.

5.3.1.2 Practical tools for Complete Model Specification

- **Eclipse Modeling Framework (EMF)**: For metamodeling and model validation.
- **Xtext** & **Sirius**: For defining DSLs and graphical editors.
- **fUML** and **Moka**: For model execution.
- **Alloy**, **SPIN**: For model checking.

5.4 Semantics (Axiomatic, Operational, Denotational)

5.4.1 Why formal semantics?

Formal semantics allows an unambiguous interpretation of models and any computational entity:

- It is the ideal theoretical basis for automated verification, execution, and code generation.
- It provides a link between the model's abstractions and the underlying computations.

5.4.2 Types of formal semantics

We distinguish three major styles of formal semantics, which are:

5.4.2.1 Axiomatic semantics

This describes system properties using logical predicates or assertions about the state of variables before and after execution. It is used to specify preconditions, postconditions, and invariants on the system.

The typical example of such semantics is the OCL language.
This semantics is used to establish correctness proofs and security property verifications.

5.4.2.2 Operational Semantics

This semantics defines the behavior of model elements during execution via transitions or state changes (often through finite state machines). It is used to interpret models and simulate their behavior.
Interpreters such as Moka use operational semantics to "execute" models.
This semantics is used for simulations, step-by-step debugging, and trace generation.

5.4.2.3 Denotational Semantics

This semantics associates each construct of a modeling language with a mathematical domain in order to reason about the behavior of a system in a compositional and abstract manner.
It is used for compositional analysis and formal equivalence proofs. In this regard, we can cite Coq and Isabelle/HOL as tools supporting denotational semantics.

5.4.3 Practical Integration in IDM

Model checking often relies on operational or denotational semantics, while model execution uses operational semantics (e.g., in fUML).
For contract-based design, axiomatic semantics are used to specify assumptions and guarantees.

5.4.4 Application Example: Model for an Elevator System

Axiomatic semantics:

"The elevator never moves with the doors open."

Operational semantics:

- ✓ **States**: {Inactive, Moving, Doors Open}
- ✓ **Transitions** triggered by events (calls and commands).

Denotational semantics:

"Behavior as a sequence of events over time. "

Chapter 6. Conclusion

Model-driven engineering (MDE) represents a paradigm shift in software and systems development, emphasizing the central role of models as primary development artifacts and design concepts rather than mere documentation. Throughout these lecture notes, I have explored the theoretical foundations, practical techniques, and technologies that make MDE a powerful approach for managing complexity, increasing automation, and ensuring correctness in modern engineering.

From Foundations to Execution

In Chapter 1, I established the fundamental principles of MDE, highlighting its motivation to combat software complexity and promote abstraction, automation, and traceability. I introduced the MDA framework, the modeling layers (from instance to metamodel), and the ecosystem of modeling languages and tools that underpin the practice of MDE. Chapter 2 focused on OCL (Object Constraint Language), a formal language essential for specifying invariants, preconditions, and postconditions regardless of the deployment platform. I examined its role in ensuring the semantic rigor of models and its integration into metamodels and transformation rules.

In **Chapter 3**, I discussed metamodeling using MOF (Meta-Object Facility). I explored how modeling languages are defined by metamodels, enabling the creation of domain-specific languages (DSLs) and promoting reusability and consistency across modeling tools.

Chapter 4 introduced the concept of model transformation, central to IDM automation. I explored the types of transformations (e.g., model-to-model and model-to-text) and how transformations operationalize the evolution, refinement, and code generation of models across development stages.

Finally, **Chapter 5** examined model execution and verification, focusing on their dynamic aspects. We explored how models can be executed, simulated, or verified using formal semantics: axiomatic, operational, and denotational. Techniques such as model checking, behavioral modeling, and executable semantics illustrated how IDM not only specifies structure but also supports validation and correctness.

The Broader Impact of IDM

IDM promotes a systematic, formal, and tool-based approach to software engineering that transcends traditional coding practices. It enables early error detection, supports automatic code generation, and facilitates platform-independent design and verification. Moreover, its application extends beyond software to areas such as embedded systems, cyber-physical systems, and digital twins.

Yet, challenges remain, particularly in terms of tool integration, transformation scalability, and maintaining alignment between models and their real-world counterparts. Advances in

AI-driven modeling, cloud-based collaborative platforms, and standardized execution semantics promise to address some of these limitations in the future.

For students…

As future engineers and researchers, your understanding of IDM will enable you to reason at higher levels of abstraction, rigorously define and manipulate models, and contribute to the next generation of model-driven intelligent systems. Whether applied in industry or academia, MDE provides a rich, formal, and scalable foundation for addressing the complexity of modern system design.

Chapter 7. References and further reading

1. **Beydeda, Sami; Book, Matthias; Gruhn, Volker**, *Model-Driven Software Development*, Springer, 2005.
2. **Brambilla, Marco; Cabot, Jordi; Wimmer, Manuel**, *Model-Driven Software Engineering in Practice*, Morgan & Claypool Publishers, 2012.
3. **Burgueño, Lola; Di Ruscio, Davide; Sahraoui, Houari; Wimmer, Manuel**, *Automation in Model-Driven Engineering: A Look Back, and Ahead*, arXiv, 2024.
4. **Clark, Tony; Warmer, Jos**, *Object Modeling with the OCL: The Rationale behind the Object Constraint Language*, Springer, 2002.
5. **Czarnecki, Krzysztof; Helsen, Simon**, *Classification of Model Transformation Approaches*, OOPSLA Workshop on Generative Techniques in the Context of Model-Driven Architecture, 2003.
6. **Di Rocco, Juri; Di Ruscio, Davide; Di Sipio, Claudio; Nguyen, Phuong T.; Rubei, Riccardo**, *On the Use of Large Language Models in Model-Driven Engineering*, arXiv, 2024.
7. **Di Ruscio, Davide; Kolovos, Dimitris; de Lara, Juan; et al.**, *Low-Code Development and Model-Driven Engineering: Two Sides of the Same Coin?*, Software and Systems Modeling, Springer, 2022.
8. **Fishwick, Paul A.**, *Simulation Model Design and Execution: Building Digital Worlds*, Prentice Hall, 1995.
9. **France, Robert B.; Rumpe, Bernhard**, *Model-Driven Development of Complex Software: A Research Roadmap*, IEEE Computer Society, 2007.
10. **Giunta, Benito; Burnay, Corentin**, *Uncovering Key Features for Model-Driven Engineering of Complex Performance Indicators: A Scoping Review*, arXiv, 2025.
11. **Kiczales, Gregor; des Rivières, Jim; Bobrow, Daniel G.**, *The Art of the Metaobject Protocol*, MIT Press, 1991.
12. **Kleppe, Anneke; Warmer, Jos; Bast, Wim**, *MDA Explained: The Model Driven Architecture: Practice and Promise*, Addison-Wesley, 2003.
13. **Lano, Kevin; Haughton, Howard; Yuan, Zhi; et al.**, *Agile Model-Driven Re-Engineering*, Innovations in Systems and Software Engineering, Springer, 2024.
14. **Mens, Tom; Van Gorp, Pieter**, *A Taxonomy of Model Transformation*, Electronic Notes in Theoretical Computer Science, Elsevier, 2006.
15. **Neureiter, Christian**, *A Domain-Specific, Model Driven Engineering Approach For Systems Engineering In The Smart Grid*, MBSE4U, 2016.

16. **Object Management Group (OMG)**, *Meta Object Facility (MOF) Core Specification, Version 2.0*, OMG, 2006.
17. **Object Management Group (OMG)**, *MOF 2.0 Facility And Object Lifecycle Specification*, OMG, 2021.
18. **Object Management Group (OMG)**, *MOF2 Versioning and Development Lifecycle*, OMG, 2007.
19. **Object Management Group (OMG)**, *MOF Model to Text Transformation Language*, OMG, 2008.
20. **Object Management Group (OMG)**, *Object Constraint Language (OCL), Version 2.4*, OMG, 2014.
21. **Ptolemaeus, Claudius (Ed.)**, *System Design, Modeling, and Simulation using Ptolemy II*, Ptolemy.org, 2014.
22. **Raza, Hammad; Deol, Esha; Hedge, Saurabh; Tanvir, Hammad**, *Model-Based Systems Engineering for Sustainable Autonomous Vehicle Design and Development*, Journal of Knowledge Learning and Science Technology, 2024.
23. **Rhazali, Yassine**, *Advancements in Model-Driven Architecture in Software Engineering*, IGI Global, 2020.
24. **Schmidt, Douglas C.**, *Guest Editor's Introduction: Model-Driven Engineering*, Computer, IEEE, 2006.
25. **Stahl, Thomas; Völter, Markus**, *Model-Driven Software Development: Technology, Engineering, Management*, Wiley, 2006.
26. **Umar, Muhammad Aminu; Lano, Kevin; Abubakar, Abdullahi Kutiriko**, *Automated Requirements Engineering Framework for Agile Model-Driven Development*, Frontiers in Computer Science, 2025.
27. **Warmer, Jos; Kleppe, Anneke**, *The Object Constraint Language: Getting Your Models Ready for MDA*, Addison-Wesley, 2003.
28. **Wiley**, *Model-Driven and Software Product Line Engineering*, Wiley, 2015.

www.ingramcontent.com/pod-product-compliance
Lightning Source LLC
LaVergne TN
LVHW082359200926
848481LV00012B/3625
9798231883141